Personal Choice

From the Library of

Personal Choice

A Poetry Anthology

edited by

JOHN WAIN

David & Charles
Newton Abbot London North Pomfret (Vt) Vancouver

Publisher's Note

This is an entirely personal anthology, a nosegay of Mr
Wain's favourite poems; it makes no attempt to 'represent'
any period or any poet. Though like any anthology it can be
used for casual dipping, the poems are arranged in an order
that (it is hoped) gives the collection a certain unity if read
from beginning to end.

All the poets and poems are listed in the indices and ac-
knowledgement of copyright permissions is at the end of the
book.

British Library Cataloguing in Publication Data
Personal Choice
   1. English poetry
   I. Wain, John
   821'.008   PR1174
   ISBN 0-7153-7505-9
Library of Congress Catalog Card Number 77-91747

Introduction and Arrangement © John Wain 1978
Copyright poems are given in the
acknowledgements at the end of the book.
All rights reserved. No part of this
publication may be reproduced, stored
in a retrieval system, or transmitted,
in any form or by any means, electronic,
mechanical, photocopying, recording or
otherwise, without the prior permission
of David & Charles (Publishers) Limited

Set in Monotype 11d on 13pt Sabon 669 series
by HBM Typesetting Limited
Standish Street Chorley Lancashire
and printed in Great Britain
by Biddles Limited Guildford
for David & Charles (Publishers) Limited
Brunel House Newton Abbot Devon

Published in the United States of America
by David & Charles Inc
North Pomfret Vermont 05053 USA

Published in Canada
by Douglas David & Charles Limited
1875 Welch Street North Vancouver BC

Introduction

One of the things I have never bothered to do is to define poetry, though I have been reading and delighting in it for so many years. One might as well try to define a poet; in fact, now that I come to think of it, I would have more confidence in trying to define a poet than in trying to define poetry. I have known many poets, some slightly, some very closely, of every age, both sexes, and many nationalities, and when I muse over what, if anything, they have in common, it seems to me that I can detect some shared, irreducible quality, some poethood, that really does unite them and mark them off from most other people. There is always, at the centre of the poet's being, a core of stillness; even poets with very anarchic lives, even poets who go mad and have to be locked up, seem to have this basic pool of tranquillity somewhere so deep inside them that the world cannot touch it; or, if the world does manage to touch and infect it, they cease to be poets. There are other, less essential, marks of poethood; many poets, for instance, have no sense of humour, though they may have a sense of boisterous fun, which is not the same thing; humour is a matter of finding amusement in the incongruity of things, and a poet is more likely to find wonder in it. Another frequent mark of the poet is a passion for information, particularly about the physical world; most of the poets I know have an astonishing knowledge of rocks, plants, birds, animals and fish. Then again, many poets are unmusical — some of the greatest of them have actually been tone-deaf — as if the verbal music that sings incessantly in their heads had the power to drown out every other kind of music. Lastly I would add that many poets are indifferent linguists. Although they spend their lives in the subtle manipulation of words, rhythms and cadences, they often have a struggle to learn any other language than their native one. Perhaps their deep involvement with the subtleties and the passionate colours of one language makes them quail before the prospect of starting it all over again with a new one.

I think, then, that I can recognize a poet. And that I can recognize a poem, as distinct from a mere construction in verse. And yet to define poetry, except in the broadest and most casual terms, seems to me unsafe. If we coin too exact a definition, and stick to it too rigorously, we shall end by screening ourselves away from some kinds of poetic experience, legislating against fine work because it seems to us 'not poetry'.

The most memorable descriptions of poetry, to my mind, have been not definitions but characterizations. The effort to define may be vain, but it is possible — it has been done — to convey in words the nature of poetry in such a way as to arouse in the reader the same kind of response as he gets from poetry itself: as when Coleridge, in one of his letters, says that the poet

> must have the ear of a wild Arab listening in the silent Desart, the eye of a North American Indian tracing the footsteps of an Enemy upon the Leaves that strew the Forest — , the Touch of a Blind Man feeling the face of a darling Child.

As a working definition, then, I would go no further than this: that poetry is to prose what dancing is to walking. Prose is the utilitarian medium that gets you from A to B. This process need not be a dreary one; a journey can be fascinating or boring, according to the kind of country it takes us through, and who our companions are, and how responsive or inert we ourselves are feeling. A prose narrative can be, in its own way, as delightful as a poem. Dancing, on the other hand, is not a means of getting somewhere, but a means of communication and expression. A couple on a dance-floor are not trying to make you think that this is their normal way of walking, nor are they going from somewhere to somewhere else; they are enjoying the music, and the rhythm, and the proximity of one another, and the movement of their limbs.

They are also liberated from fatigue; in the course of an evening's dancing, they will cover more miles than they would unprotestingly walk in a day. They are giving one another something that they could never give by merely walking along together; and of course, *mutatis mutandis*, this applies equally well to dances performed by a group, or to a *pas seul*.

In the same way, though it is perfectly possible to convey information or tell a story in poetry, those are not its primary uses. The poet is not inviting his reader to come on a journey, but to join in a dance. And he is not trying to make out that poetry is his normal way of talking. There has been, for the last fifty years and more, a widespread view that poetry ought to sound like conversation; yet it is not conversation, and is not intended to serve the same purposes, so I do not see why it should obey the same laws.

Many societies have endowed the poet with a magical or priestly function; they have made little distinction between the poem, designed to engage the emotions and to relate high events, and the rune, the curse or blessing, the prayer, the spell. There are many ages and nations from which we might fetch our examples, but if we are to select one, let it be ancient Ireland, where we read that the word 'druid', like the Latin *vates*, is frequently a synonym for 'poet', the poet being credited with the same wizardry as the druid. In the tenth-century glossary of King Cormac, there is a description of the method used by the poet to perceive far-off events in time and space. It was done by means of an incantation called *Imbas Forosnai*. The poet chewed a piece of the raw flesh of a pig, a dog or a cat, then retired with it to his bed behind the door, pronounced an oration over it and offered it to his gods. If by the next day the gods had not vouchsafed illumination, the poet pronounced certain incantations over the palms of his hands, laid his hands across his cheeks, and went into a trance-like sleep. It was forbidden to disturb him during this sleep, which might last for days, and at the end of which he would have the required vision. Another incantation or *Cétnad* was used for detecting a theft. This was sung through

7

the right fist on the track of the stolen beast (note the assumption, doubtless correct, that the only things worth stealing in that society were horses and cattle), or on the track of the thief, if the animal was dead. Three times should be enough to find the right track, but if the stolen animal was not discovered, one sang it a further time, still through the right fist, and then slept; and in that sleep the thief would be seen and known.

Clearly such magical powers were not acquired cheaply. The poet resembled the druid not only in powers and privilleges, but in the length and ferocity of that apprenticeship which showed his dedication. The Bardic Schools, which we learn about in the Synod of Drumceat in 590 and which continued until the seventeenth century, required of the aspiring poet a body of esoteric knowledge that might take twenty years to master. There were six poetic titles or degrees: *focloc, macfuirmedh, doss, cana, cli, anradh, ollamh*. What these involved I have no idea, but they indicate a training and a status within the community that were objectified and recognized. The Bardic Schools were grouped, not round localities, but round personalities; each school mustered about a chief poet who wandered where the fancy took him, and wherever they appeared they were welcomed and supported by the population. Small wonder, for the bards were powerful figures, able to protect or to destroy. One *Cétnad* which the apprentice poet learnt by heart was addressed to 'the seven daughters of the sea, who shape the thread of long-lived children,' and brought length of life. Another was the *Glam dichinn*, in which the poet punished a king who refused patronage that had been fairly earned. This was an elaborate commination performed by seven poets at once; according to the description in Douglas Hyde's *A Literary History of Ireland*, the punitive band

> went at the rising of the sun to a hill which should be situated on the boundary of seven lands, and each of them was to turn his face to a different land, and the *ollamh's* (ollav's) face was to be turned to the land of the

king, who was to be satirised, and their backs should be turned to a hawthorn which should be growing upon the top of a hill, and the wind should be blowing from the north, and each man was to hold a perforated stone and a thorn of the hawthorn in his hand, and each man was to sing a verse of this composition for the king — the *ollamh* or chief poet to take the lead with his own verse, and the others in concert after him with theirs; and each then should place his stone and his thorn under the stem of the hawthorn, and if it was they that were in the wrong in the case, the ground of the hill would swallow them, and if it was the king that was in the wrong, the ground would swallow him and his wife, and his son and his steed, and his robes and his hound. The satire of the *macfuirmedh* fell on the hound, the satire of the *focloc* on the robes, the satire of the *doss* on the arms, the satire of the *cana* on the wife, the satire of the *cli* on the son, the satire of the *anrad* on the steed, the satire of the *ollamh* on the king.

At first glance, nothing could be further from our attitudes today. Modern urban society has banished the idea of magic; as Cyril Connolly put it in *The Unquiet Grave,*

It is a significant comment on the victory of science over magic that were someone to say 'if I put this pill in your beer it will explode,' we might believe them; but were they to cry 'if I pronounce this spell over your beer it will go flat,' we should remain incredulous and Paracelsus, the Alchemists, Aleister Crowley and all the Magi have lived in vain.

'Yet,' Connolly added, 'when I read science I turn magical; when I study magic, scientific.' He touched here, one feels, on a widespread reaction; there are times when not only the latest triumphs of scientific research but the most familiar products of technology — an electric torch, for instance — seem miraculous and magical. The formal study of magic is almost completely dead in our society, yet the atmosphere of magic lingers on in corners of the human mind. Certainly something of the magical, or at any rate the supernatural, clings to the idea of the poet. It is he, and not the novelist or playwright, who takes the skills of language to the frontiers of rationality and beyond. The most hard-headed modern people expect of a poet some power of perception, as well as of expression, beyond the ordinary human range. A poem is still a kind of rune or spell or prayer. Not surprisingly, for the poet does more than any other artist to release the power that is latent in language; and language is such a miraculous achievement that we might easily consider it akin to the magical.

Homo sapiens is marked off from the other creatures primarily by the power of speech. Even the dolphin, which has a more complex brain than our own, does not compile dictionaries. The Book of Genesis tells us that Adam's first task was to name the animals, and it has remained true that the primary human faculty has been to order experience by means of language; to order it, and to store it. Every people that invents a language engages in a collective act of creativity that dwarfs the achievement of any individual artist, even a Shakespeare. Language stores the impressions, the thoughts, the emotions of an entire race. Its latent power is immense. But most users of any language are like children picking out the notes of a grand piano with one chubby finger. The music is there, but only the trained and gifted performer can bring it out. Any writer worthy of the name releases a significant amount of the energy that is contained within language, but only the poet releases it at its highest intensity. To do this he uses a variety of technical means that move speech away from ordinary conversation, or utilitarian prose, and bring it towards song, dance, incantation. The achieved poem gives back to the people the stored-up emotional and imaginative power that came from the people in the first instance. Hence the poet 'speaks for' his nation, and for humanity in general, more fully than any other artist. The visual artist uses colours and shapes, the musician uses sounds, all of which already existed in nature. But words did not exist in nature: humanity made them, and stored its collective life in them like the marrow in bones. Only the poet can bring that life back into the world and make it part of our daily experience. And if this is not magic, it is as close to magic as makes no difference.

In this selection, I have been guided solely by my own pleasure. These are not *all* the poems I enjoy (a dozen volumes would be needed for that), but there is no poem here that I do not enjoy. As regards editorial principle, I made only two rules: not to include any prose poetry, and to present whole poems rather than extracts. Both these rules I broke at once. Many of the finest poems are simply too long to be included, yet contain passages I re-read as I re-read single poems. Some of these passages I give here, though I am perfectly well aware that they are even better in their natural setting. And in selecting some passages from Shakespeare — which I can only hope don't appear as bleeding chunks — I found I could not leave out the voice of Falstaff, though he speaks in prose, nor Mistress Quickly's lament over his death, which has the Shakespearean combination of humour and pathos, and is as charged with the imaginative power of a great poet as anything he wrote in verse.

In other words, I have been inconsistent, just as I have in the matter of original spelling. As a broad rule, all poets up to the mid-sixteenth century appear in their own (or their printers') spelling; from then until the eighteenth century, the spelling is modernized; after the early years of that century, the differences are too slight to matter much, and I used any good text that was conveniently to hand. The inconsistencies, and breakings of the rule, are immediately obvious; indeed I hope they are, since the more obvious they are the less they will mislead. It seems to me, for instance, absurd to print Shakespeare in the spelling of the Quartos and Folios; whereas Milton, who had a scholar's concern for orthography perhaps frustrated by a blind man's inability to enforce it, looks (to my eye) all wrong in modern spelling. I have followed my own preference, being irresponsible and in holiday mood; but in two important respects I have played fair with the reader. First, I have used no corrupt and garbled versions, but only texts vouched for by reputable scholars and brought out by publishers with a reputation to lose; second, if I print a poem as complete it *is* complete, with no unannounced gaps or silent omissions. (You would be surprised, until you looked into it, how many distinguished anthologists trim the poems they present, like a butcher making a joint of meat look more appetizing, or dog-owner preparing his pet for Cruft's.) If any poem in this book is excerpted or shortened in any way, it announces the fact.

So much for explanations, and now let the poets speak.

John Wain
Autumn 1977

Personal Choice

To Oxford

(i)

New-dated from the terms that reappear,
More sweet-familiar grows my love to thee,
And still thou bind'st me to fresh fealty
With long-superfluous ties, for nothing here
Nor elsewhere can thy sweetness unendear.
This is my park, my pleasaunce; this to me
As public is my greater privacy,
All mine, yet common to my every peer.
Those charms accepted of my inmost thought,
The towers musical, quiet-walled grove,
The window-circles, these may all be sought
By other eyes, and other suitors move,
And all like me may boast, impeached not,
Their special-general title to thy love.

(ii)

Thus, I come underneath this chapel-side,
So that the mason's levels, courses, all
The vigorous horizontals, each way fall
In bows above my head, as falsified
By visual compulsion, till I hide
The steep-up roof at last behind the small
Eclipsing parapet; yet above the wall
The sumptuous ridge-crest leave to poise and ride.
None besides me this bye-ways beauty try.
Or if they try it, I am happier then:
The shapen flags and drillèd holes of sky,
Just seen, may be to many unknown men
The one peculiar of their pleasured eye,
And I have only set the same to pen.

GERARD MANLEY HOPKINS

From Thyrsis

Well! wind-dispersed and vain the words will be,
  Yet, Thyrsis, let me give my grief its hour
    In the old haunt, and find our tree-topped hill!
  Who, if not I, for questing here hath power?
    I know the wood which hides the daffodil,
      I know the Fyfield tree,
  I know what white, what purple fritillaries
    The grassy harvest of the river-fields,
    Above by Ensham, down by Sandford, yields,
  And what sedged brooks are Thames's tributaries;

I know these slopes; who knows them if not I?—
  But many a dingle on the loved hill-side,
    With thorns once studded, old, white-blossomed trees,
  Where thick the cowslips grew, and far descried
    High towered the spikes of purple orchises,
      Hath since our day put by
  The coronals of that forgotten time;
    Down each green bank hath gone the ploughboy's team,
    And only in the hidden brookside gleam
  Primroses, orphans of the flowery prime.

Where is the girl, who by the boatman's door,
  Above the locks, above the boating throng,
    Unmoored our skiff when through the Wytham flats,
  Red loosestrife and blond meadow-sweet among
    And darting swallows and light water-gnats,
      We tracked the shy Thames shore?
  Where are the mowers, who, as the tiny swell
    Of our boat passing heaved the river-grass,
    Stood with suspended scythe to see us pass?—
  They all are gone, and thou art gone as well!

MATTHEW ARNOLD

In Memoriam

(VII)

Dark house, by which once more I stand
   Here in the long unlovely street,
   Doors, where my heart was used to beat
So quickly, waiting for a hand,

A hand that can be clasped no more—
   Behold me, for I cannot sleep,
   And like a guilty thing I creep
At earliest morning to the door.

He is not here; but far away
   The noise of life begins again,
   And ghastly through the drizzling rain
On the bald street breaks the blank day.

ALFRED, LORD TENNYSON

To the Memory of Mr. Oldham

Farewel, too little and too lately known,
Whom I began to think and call my own;
For sure our Souls were near ally'd; and thine
Cast in the same Poetick mould with mine.
One common Note on either Lyre did strike,
And Knaves and Fools we both abhorr'd alike:
To the same Goal did both our Studies drive,
The last set out the soonest did arrive.
Thus *Nisus* fell upon the slippery place,
While his young Friend perform'd and won the Race.
O early ripe! to thy abundant store
What could advancing Age have added more?
It might (what Nature never gives the young)
Have taught the numbers of thy native Tongue.

17

But Satyr needs not those, and Wit will shine
Through the harsh cadence of a rugged line.
A noble Error, and but seldom made,
When Poets are by too much force betray'd.
Thy generous fruits, though gather'd ere their prime
Still shew'd a quickness; and maturing time
But mellows what we write to the dull sweets of Rime.
Once more, hail and farewel; farewel thou young,
But ah too short, *Marcellus* of our Tongue;
Thy Brows with Ivy, and with Laurels bound;
But Fate and gloomy Night encompass thee around.

JOHN DRYDEN

Seferis

Time quietly compiling us like sheaves
Turns round one day, beckons the special few,
With one bird singing somewhere in the leaves,
Someone like K. or somebody like you,
Free-falling target for the envious thrust,
So tilting into darkness go we must.

Thus the fading writer signing off
Sees in the vast perspectives of dispersal
His words float off like tiny seeds,
Wind-borne or bird-distributed notes,
To the very end of loves without rehearsal,
The stinging image riper than his deeds.

Yours must have set out like ancient
Colonists, from Delos or from Rhodes,
To dare the sun-gods, found great entrepôts,
Naples or Rio, far from man's known abodes,
To confer the quaint Grecian script on other men;
A new Greek fire ignited by your pen.

How marvellous to have done it and then left
It in the lost property office of the loving mind,
The secret whisper those who listen find.
You show us all the way the great ones went,
In silences becalmed, so well they knew
That even to die is somehow to invent.

LAWRENCE DURRELL

Extempore Effusion Upon the Death of James Hogg

When first, descending from the moorlands,
 I saw the Stream of Yarrow glide
Along a bare and open valley,
 The Ettrick Shepherd was my guide.

When last along its banks I wandered,
Through groves that had begun to shed
Their golden leaves upon the pathways,
My steps the Border-minstrel led.

The mighty Minstrel breathes no longer,
'Mid mouldering ruins low he lies;
And death upon the braes of Yarrow,
Has closed the Shepherd-poet's eyes:

Nor has the rolling year twice measured,
From sign to sign, its steadfast course,
Since every mortal power of Coleridge
Was frozen at its marvellous source;

The rapt One, of the godlike forehead,
The heaven-eyed creature sleeps in earth:
And Lamb, the frolic and the gentle,
Has vanished from his lonely hearth.

Like clouds that rake the mountain-summits,
Or waves that own no curbing hand,
How fast has brother followed brother,
From sunshine to the sunless land!

Yet I, whose lids from infant slumber
Were earlier raised, remain to hear
A timid voice, that asks in whispers,
"Who next will drop and disappear?"

Our haughty life is crowned with darkness,
Like London with its own black wreath,
On which with thee, O Crabbe! forthlooking,
I gazed from Hampstead's breezy heath.

As if but yesterday departed,
Thou too art gone before; but why,
O'er ripe fruit, seasonably gathered,
Should frail survivors heave a sigh?

Mourn rather for that holy Spirit,
Sweet as the spring, as ocean deep;
For Her who, ere her summer faded,
Has sunk into a breathless sleep.

No more of old romantic sorrows,
For slaughtered Youth or love-lorn Maid!
With sharper grief is Yarrow smitten,
And Ettrick mourns with her their Poet dead.

WILLIAM WORDSWORTH

On Sitting Down to Read King Lear Once Again

O golden tongued Romance, with serene lute!
  Fair plumed Syren, Queen of far-away!
  Leave melodizing on this wintry day,
Shut up thine olden pages, and be mute:
Adieu! for, once again, the fierce dispute
  Betwixt damnation and impassion'd clay
  Must I burn through; once more humbly assay
The bitter-sweet of this Shakespearian fruit:

Chief Poet! and ye clouds of Albion,
  Begetters of our deep eternal theme!
When through the old oak Forest I am gone,
  Let me not wander in a barren dream,
But, when I am consumed in the fire,
Give me new Phœnix wings to fly at my desire.

JOHN KEATS

Songs of Experience

Introduction

Hear the voice of the Bard!
Who Present, Past, and Future, sees;
Whose ears have heard
The Holy Word
That walk'd among the ancient trees,

Calling the lapsèd Soul,
And weeping in the evening dew;
That might controll
The starry pole,
And fallen, fallen light renew!

'O Earth, O Earth, return!
Arise from out the dewy grass;
Night is worn,
And the morn
Rises from the slumberous mass.

'Turn away no more;
Why wilt thou turn away?
The starry floor,
The wat'ry shore,
Is giv'n thee till the break of day.'

WILLIAM BLAKE

Maîtresses de Mon Coeur

Maîtresses de mon coeur, incomparables Fées,
Par qui les héros morts sont des héros vivants,
Notre siècle a cessé de suivre les Orphées,
Un guerrier lui plait mieux qu'un peuple de savants.

Vous avez beau chanter, vous trouvez peu d'oreilles
Qui se laissent ravir à vos charmantes voix;
Et bien que mes rivaux produisent des merveilles,
On leur ouvre à regret le Cabinet des Rois.

Muses, que deviendrait l'honneur de votre bande,
Si Séguier de qui l'âme est si juste et si grande,
Appuyait faiblement ceux qui vous font l'amour?

En ce temps où la guerre afflige tant d'empires
Le bruit de la trompette et le bruit des tambours
Imposeraient silence au concert de nos lyres.

FRANÇOIS MAYNARD

From Paradise Lost (Book I)

Of Mans First Disobedience, and the Fruit
Of that Forbidden Tree, whose mortal tast
Brought Death into the World, and all our woe,
With loss of *Eden*, till one greater Man
Restore us, and regain the blissful Seat,
Sing Heav'nly Muse, that on the secret top
Of *Oreb*, or of *Sinai*, didst inspire
That Shepherd, who first taught the chosen Seed,
In the Beginning how the Heav'ns and Earth
Rose out of *Chaos*: Or if *Sion* Hill
Delight thee more, and *Siloa's* Brook that flow'd
Fast by the Oracle of God; I thence
Invoke thy aid to my adventrous Song,
That with no middle flight intends to soar
Above th' *Aonian* Mount, while it pursues
Things unattempted yet in Prose or Rhime.
And chiefly Thou O Spirit, that dost prefer
Before all Temples th' upright heart and pure,
Instruct me, for Thou know'st; Thou from the first
Wast present, and with mighty wings outspread
Dove-like satst brooding on the vast Abyss
And mad'st it pregnant: What in me is dark
Illumine, what is low raise and support;
That to the highth of this great Argument
I may assert Eternal Providence,
And justifie the wayes of God to men.

JOHN MILTON

23

To R. B.

The fine delight that fathers thought; the strong
Spur, live and lancing like the blowpipe flame,
Breathes once and, quenchèd faster than it came,
Leaves yet the mind a mother of immortal song.
Nine months she then, nay years, nine years she long
Within her wears, bears, cares and moulds the same:
The widow of an insight lost she lives, with aim
Now known and hand at work now never wrong.
　　Sweet fire the sire of muse, my soul needs this;
I want the one rapture of an inspiration.
O then if in my lagging lines you miss
The roll, the rise, the carol, the creation,
My winter world, that scarcely breathes that bliss
Now, yields you, with some sighs, our explanation.

GERARD MANLEY HOPKINS

The Break of Day and the Falling of Night

The break of day and the falling of night
birds fish moths in their generations
come without date: there is no infinite:
sea, rock and fossil are my creations.

Poetry without time is a sun-flame
flickering on the misty sea-surface
conversation has always been the same,
seen naked its body has strength and grace:

and I consider I have no future
but sea-blasted roses and foreshore grass,
the strongest languages are most impure,
I wear love on my chest like a horse-brass.

O unwritten poem, secret mountain
peaks, bogmyrtle, bracken and idle men,
handfuls of birds in handfuls of rain,
repeat these words once and forget them then.

PETER LEVI

The Choice

The intellect of man is forced to choose
Perfection of the life, or of the work,
And if it take the second must refuse
A heavenly mansion, raging in the dark.

When all that story's finished, what's the news?
In luck or out the toil has left its mark:
That old perplexity an empty purse,
Or the day's vanity, the night's remorse.

W. B. YEATS

From Paradise Lost (Book VII)

The Argument

Descend from Heav'n *Urania*, by that name
If rightly thou art call'd, whose Voice divine
Following, above th' *Olympian* Hill I soare,
Above the flight of *Pegasean* wing.
The meaning, not the Name I call: for thou
Nor of the Muses nine, nor on the top
Of old *Olympus* dwell'st, but Heav'nlie borne,
Before the Hills appeerd, or Fountain flow'd,
Thou with Eternal wisdom didst converse,

Wisdom thy Sister, and with her didst play
In presence of th' Almightie Father, pleas'd
With thy Celestial Song. Up led by thee
Into the Heav'n of Heav'ns I have presum'd,
An Earthlie Guest, and drawn Empyreal Aire,
Thy tempring; with like safetie guided down
Return me to my Native Element:
Least from this flying Steed unrein'd, (as once
Bellerophon, though from a lower Clime)
Dismounted, on th' *Aleian* Field I fall
Erroneous, there to wander and forlorne.
Half yet remaines unsung, but narrower bound
Within the visible Diurnal Spheare;
Standing on Earth, not rapt above the Pole,
More safe I Sing with mortal voice, unchang'd
To hoarce or mute, though fall'n on evil dayes,
On evil dayes though fall'n, and evil tongues;
In darkness, and with dangers compast round,
And solitude; yet not alone, while thou
Visit'st my slumbers Nightly, or when Morn
Purples the East: still govern thou my Song,
Urania, and fit audience find, though few.
But drive farr off the barbarous dissonance
Of *Bacchus* and his Revellers, the Race
Of that wilde Rout that tore the *Thracian* Bard
In *Rhodope*, where Woods and Rocks had Eares
To rapture, till the savage clamor dround
Both Harp and Voice; nor could the Muse defend
Her Son.   So fail not thou, who thee implores:
For thou art Heav'nlie, shee an empty dreame.

JOHN MILTON

I am Taliesin. I sing perfect metre

I am Taliesin. I sing perfect metre,
Which will last to the end of the world.
My patron is Elphin . . .

I know why there is an echo in a hollow;
Why silver gleams; why breath is black; why liver is bloody;
Why a cow has horns; why a woman is affectionate;
Why milk is white; why holly is green;
Why a kid is bearded; why the cow-parsnip is hollow;
Why brine is salt; why ale is bitter;
Why the linnet is green and berries red;
Why a cuckoo complains; why it sings;

I know where the cuckoos of summer are in winter.
I know what beasts there are at the bottom of the sea;
How many spears in battle; how many drops in a shower;
Why a river drowned Pharaoh's people;
Why fishes have scales,
Why a white swan has black feet . . .

I have been a blue salmon,
I have been a dog, a stag, a roebuck on the mountain,
A stock, a spade, an axe in the hand,
A stallion, a bull, a buck,
A grain which grew on a hill,
I was reaped, and placed in an oven,
I fell to the ground when I was being roasted
And a hen swallowed me.
For nine nights was I in her crop.
I have been dead, I have been alive,
I am Taliesin.

13TH CENTURY MS
TRANSLATED FROM THE WELSH
BY IFOR WILLIAMS

Tom o' Bedlam

From the hag and hungry goblin
That into rags would rend ye,
The spirit that stands by the naked man
In the Book of Moons defend ye,
That of your five sound senses
You never be forsaken,
Nor wander from yourselves with Tom
Abroad to beg your bacon,
    While I do sing, Any food, any feeding,
    Feeding, drink, or clothing;
    Come dame or maid, be not afraid,
    Poor Tom will injure nothing.

Of thirty bare years have I
Twice twenty been enragèd,
And of forty been three times fifteen
In durance soundly cagèd
On the lordly lofts of Bedlam
With stubble soft and dainty,
Brave bracelets strong, sweet whips ding dong
With wholesome hunger plenty,
    And now I sing, etc.

With a thought I took for Maudlin
And a cruse of cockle pottage,
With a thing thus tall, sky bless you all,
I befell into this dotage.
I slept not since the Conquest,
Till then I never wakèd,
Till the roguish boy of love where I lay
Me found and strip't me naked.
    And now I sing, etc.

When I short have shorn my sow's face
And swigged my horny barrel,
In an oaken inn I pound my skin
As a suit of gilt apparel;
The moon's my constant mistress
And the lovely owl my marrow;
The flaming drake and the night crow make
Me music to my sorrow.
      While I do sing, etc.

The palsy plagues my pulses
When I prig your pigs or pullen,
Your culvers take, or matchless make
Your Chanticleer or Sullen.
When I want provant with Humphrey
I sup, and when benighted,
I repose in Paul's with waking souls
Yet never am affrighted.
      But I do sing, etc.

I know more than Apollo,
For oft when he lies sleeping
I see the stars at bloody wars
In the wounded welkin weeping;
The moon embrace her shepherd,
And the Queen of Love her warrior,
While the first doth horn the star of morn,
And the next the heavenly Farrier.
      While I do sing, etc.

The gypsies, Snap and Pedro,
Are none of Tom's comradoes,
The punk I scorn and the cutpurse sworn,
And the roaring boy's bravadoes.
The meek, the white, the gentle
Me handle, touch, and spare not;
But those that cross Tom Rynosseross
  Do what the panther dare not.
      Although I sing, etc.

With an host of furious fancies
Whereof I am commander,
With a burning spear and a horse of air,
To the wilderness I wander.
By a knight of ghosts and shadows
I summoned am to a tourney
Ten leagues beyond the wide world's end:
Methinks it is no journey.
       Yet will I sing, etc.

ANON *c*1620

King Lear (Act III, sc iv)

KENT: Here is the place, my lord; good my lord, enter.
The tyranny of the open night's too rough
For nature to endure.
LEAR: Let me alone.
KENT: Good my lord, enter here.
LEAR: Wilt break my heart?
KENT: I had rather break mine own.
        Good my lord, enter.
LEAR: Thou think'st 'tis much that this contentious
        storm
Invades us to the skin; so 'tis to thee,
But where the greater malady is fix'd,
The lesser is scarce felt. Thou'dst shun a bear;
But if thy flight lay toward the roaring sea,
Thou'dst meet the bear i' th' mouth. When the mind's free
The body's delicate; this tempest in my mind
Doth from my senses take all feeling else,
Save what beats there. Filial ingratitude!
Is it not as this mouth should tear this hand
For lifting food to't? But I will punish home.
No, I will weep no more. In such a night,

To shut me out! Pour on; I will endure.
In such a night as this! O Regan, Goneril!
Your old kind father, whose frank heart gave all!
O, that way madness lies; let me shun that;
No more of that.
KENT: Good my lord, enter here.
LEAR: Prithee go in thyself; seek thine own ease.
This tempest will not give me leave to ponder
On things would hurt me more. But I'll go in.
[*To the Fool*] In, boy; go first.—You houseless poverty—
Nay, get thee in. I'll pray, and then I'll sleep.   [*Exit Fool.*
Poor naked wretches, wheresoe'er you are,
That bide the pelting of this pitiless storm,
How shall your houseless heads and unfed sides,
Your loop'd and window'd raggedness, defend you
From seasons such as these? O, I have ta'en
Too little care of this! Take physic, pomp;
Expose thyself to feel what wretches feel,
That thou mayst shake the superflux to them.
And show the heavens more just.

WILLIAM SHAKESPEARE

Leaves of Grass

(37)

You laggards there on guard! look to your arms!
In at the conquer'd doors they crowd! I am possess'd!
Embody all presences outlaw'd or suffering,
See myself in prison shaped like another man,
And feel the dull unintermitted pain.

For me the keepers of convicts shoulder their carbines and
  keep watch,
It is I let out in the morning and barr'd at night.

Not a mutineer walks handcuff'd to jail but I am
  handcuff'd to him and walk by his side,
(I am less the jolly one there, and more the silent one with
  sweat on my twitching lips.)

Not a youngster is taken for larceny but I go up too, and
  am tried and sentenced.

Not a cholera patient lies at the last gasp but I also lie at
  the last gasp,
My face is ash-color'd, my sinews gnarl, away from me
  people retreat.

Askers embody themselves in me and I am embodied in
  them,
I project my hat, sit shame-faced, and beg.

WALT WHITMAN

Childe Harold

(CXL)

I see before me the Gladiator lie:
He leans upon his hand—his manly brow
Consents to death, but conquers agony,
And his droop'd head sinks gradually low—
And through his side the last drops, ebbing slow
From the red gash, fall heavy, one by one,
Like the first of a thunder-shower; and now
The arena swims around him—he is gone,
Ere ceased the inhuman shout which hail'd the wretch
     who won.

(CXLI)

He heard it, but he heeded not—his eyes
Were with his heart, and that was far away;
He reck'd not of the life he lost nor prize,
But where his rude hut by the Danube lay,
There were his young barbarians all at play,
There was their Dacian mother—he, their sire,
Butcher'd to make a Roman holiday—
All this rush'd with his blood—Shall he expire
And unavenged? Arise! ye Goths, and glut your ire!

LORD BYRON

Leaves of Grass

(10)

The runaway slave came to my house and stopt outside,
I heard his motions crackling the twigs of the woodpile,
Through the swung half-door of the kitchen I saw him
    limpsy and weak,
And went where he sat on a log and led him in and assured
    him,
And brought water and fill'd a tub for his sweated body
    and bruis'd feet,
And gave him a room that enter'd from my own, and gave
    him some coarse clean clothes,
And remember perfectly well his revolving eyes and his
    awkwardness,
And remember putting plasters on the galls of his neck and
    ankles;
He staid with me a week before he was recuperated and
    pass'd north,
I had him sit next me at table, my fire-lock lean'd in the
    corner.

WALT WHITMAN

L'Epitaphe Villon

Freres humains qui après nous vivez,
N'ayez les cuers contre nous endurcis,
Car, se pitié de nous povres avez,
Dieu en aura plus tost de vous mercis.
Vous nous voiez cy attachez cinq, six:
Quant de la chair, que trop avons nourrie,
Elle est pieça devorée et pourrie,
Et nous, les os, devenons cendre et pouldre.
De nostre mal personne ne s'en rie;
Mais priez Dieu que tous nous vueille absouldre!

34

Se freres vous clamons, pas n'en devez
Avoir desdaing, quoy que fusmes occis
Par justice. Toutesfois, vous sçavez
Que tous hommes n'ont pas bon sens rassis;
Excusez nous, puis que sommes transsis,
Envers le fils de la Vierge Marie,
Que sa grace ne soit pour nous tarie,
Nous preservant de l'infernale fouldre.
Nous sommes mors, ame ne nous harie;
Mais priez Dieu que tous nous vueille absouldre!

La pluye nous a debuez et lavez,
Et le soleil dessechiez et noircis;
Pies, corbeaulx, nous ont les yeux cavez,
Et arrachié la barbe et les sourcis.
Jamais nul temps nous ne sommes assis;
Puis ça, puis la, comme le vent varie,
A son plaisir sans cesser nous charie,
Plus becquetez d'oiseaulx que dez a couldre.
Ne soiez donc de nostre confrairie;
Mais priez Dieu que tous nous vueille absouldre!

Prince Jhesus, qui sur tous a maistrie,
Gar de qu'Enfer n'ait de nous seigneurie:
A luy n'ayons que faire ne que souldre.
Hommes, icy n'a point de mocquerie;
Mais priez Dieu que tous nous vueille absouldre!

FRANÇOIS VILLON

From the Ancyent Marinere

'I fear thee, ancyent Marinere!
  'I fear thy skinny hand;
'And thou art long and lank and brown
  'As is the ribb'd Sea-sand.

'I fear thee and thy glittering eye
  'And thy skinny hand so brown'—
Fear not, fear not, thou wedding guest!
  This body dropt not down.

Alone, alone, all all alone
  Alone on the wide wide Sea;
And Christ would take no pity on
  My soul in agony.

The many men so beautiful,
  And they all dead did lie!
And a million million slimy things
  Liv'd on—and so did I.

I look'd upon the rotting Sea,
  And drew my eyes away;
I look'd upon the eldritch deck,
  And there the dead men lay.

I look'd to Heaven, and try'd to pray;
  But or ever a prayer had gusht,
A wicked whisper came and made
  My heart as dry as dust.

I clos'd my lids and kept them close,
  Till the balls like pulses beat;
For the sky and the sea, and the sea and the sky
Lay like a load on my weary eye,
  And the dead were at my feet.

The cold sweat melted from their limbs,
    Ne rot, ne reek did they;
The look with which they look'd on me,
    Had never pass'd away.

An orphan's curse would drag to Hell
    A spirit from on high:
But O! more horrible than that
    Is the curse in a dead man's eye!
Seven days, seven nights I saw that curse,
    And yet I could not die.

The moving Moon went up the sky
    And no where did abide:
Softly she was going up
    And a star or two beside—

Her beams bemock'd the sultry main
    Like morning frosts yspread;
But where the ship's huge shadow lay,
The charmed water burnt alway
    A still and awful red.

Beyond the shadow of the ship
    I watch'd the water-snakes:
They mov'd in tracks of shining white;
And when they rear'd, the elfish light
    Fell off in hoary flakes.

Within the shadow of the ship
    I watch'd their rich attire:
Blue, glossy green, and velvet black
They coil'd and swam; and every track
    Was a flash of golden fire.

O happy living things! no tongue
  Their beauty might declare:
A spring of love gusht from my heart,
  And I bless'd them unaware!
Sure my kind saint took pity on me,
  And I bless'd them unaware.

The self-same moment I could pray;
  And from my neck so free
The Albatross fell off, and sank
  Like lead into the sea.

S. T. COLERIDGE

As Kingfishers Catch Fire

As kingfishers catch fire, dragonflies dráw fláme;
As tumbled over rim in roundy wells
Stones ring; like each tucked string tells, each hung bell's
Bow swung finds tongue to fling out broad its name;
Each mortal thing does one thing and the same:
Deals out that being indoors each one dwells;
Selves—goes itself; *myself* it speaks and spells,
Crying *Whát I do is me: for that I came.*

I say móre: the just man justices;
Kéeps gráce: thát keeps all his goings graces;
Acts in God's eye what in God's eye he is—
Chríst—for Christ plays in ten thousand places,
Lovely in limbs, and lovely in eyes not his
To the Father through the features of men's faces.

GERARD MANLEY HOPKINS

King Lear (Act V, sc iii)

LEAR: No, no, no, no! Come, let's away to prison.
       We two alone will sing like birds i' th' cage;
       When thou dost ask me blessing, I'll kneel down
       And ask of thee forgiveness; so we'll live,
       And pray, and sing, and tell old tales, and laugh
       At gilded butterflies, and hear poor rogues
       Talk of court news; and we'll talk with them
           too—
       Who loses and who wins; who's in, who's out—
       And take upon's the mystery of things
       As if we were God's spies; and we'll wear out
       In a wall'd prison packs and sects of great ones
       That ebb and flow by th' moon.
EDMUND: Take them away.
LEAR: Upon such sacrifices, my Cordelia,
       The gods themselves throw incense. Have I
           caught thee?
       He that parts us shall bring a brand from heaven
       And fire us hence like foxes.

WILLIAM SHAKESPEARE

Leaves of Grass

(6)

A child said *What is the grass?* fetching it to me with full
    hands;
How could I answer the child? I do not know what it is
    any more than he.

I guess it must be the flag of my disposition, out of hopeful
    green stuff woven.

39

Or I guess it is the handkerchief of the Lord,
A scented gift and remembrancer designedly dropt,
Bearing the owner's name someway in the corners, that we
may see and remark, and say *Whose?*

Or I guess the grass is itself a child, the produced babe of
the vegetation.

Or I guess it is a uniform hieroglyphic,
And it means, Sprouting alike in broad zones and narrow
zones,
Growing among black folks as among white,
Kanuck, Tuckahoe, Congressman, Cuff, I give them the
same, I receive them the same.

And now it seems to me the beautiful uncut hair of graves.

Tenderly will I use you curling grass,
It may be you transpire from the breasts of young men,
It may be if I had known them I would have loved them,
It may be you are from old people, or from offspring taken
soon out of their mothers' laps,
And here you are the mothers' laps.

This grass is very dark to be from the white heads of old
mothers,
Darker than the colorless beards of old men,
Dark to come from under the faint red roofs of mouths.

O I perceive after all so many uttering tongues,
And I perceive they do not come from the roofs of mouths
for nothing.

I wish I could translate the hints about the dead young men
and women,

And the hints about old men and mothers, and the offspring
taken soon out of their laps.

What do you think has become of the young and old men?
And what do you think has become of the women and
    children?

They are alive and well somewhere,
The smallest sprout shows there is really no death,
And if ever there was it led forward life, and does not wait
    at the end to arrest it,
And ceas'd the moment life appear'd.

All goes onward and outward, nothing collapses,
And to die is different from what any one supposed, and
    luckier.

WALT WHITMAN

Spring and Fall:

to a young child

Márgarét, are you gríeving
Over Goldengrove unleaving?
Leáves, like the things of man, you
With your fresh thoughts care for, can you?
Áh! ás the heart grows older
It will come to such sights colder
By and by, nor spare a sigh
Though worlds of wanwood leafmeal lie;
And yet you wíll weep and know why.
Now no matter, child, the name:
Sórrow's spríngs áre the same.
Nor mouth had, no nor mind, expressed
What heart heard of, ghost guessed:
It ís the blight man was born for,
It is Margaret you mourn for.

GERARD MANLEY HOPKINS

Miranda

My Dear One is mine as mirrors are lonely,
As the poor and sad are real to the good king,
And the high green hill sits always by the sea.

Up jumped the Black Man behind the elder tree,
Turned a somersault and ran away waving;
My Dear One is mine as mirrors are lonely.

The Witch gave a squawk; her venomous body
Melted into light as water leaves a spring
And the high green hill sits always by the sea.

At his crossroads, too, the Ancient prayed for me;
Down his wasted cheeks tears of joy were running:
My Dear One is mine as mirrors are lonely.

He kissed me awake, and no one was sorry;
The sun shone on sails, eyes, pebbles, anything,
And the high green hill sits always by the sea.

So, to remember our changing garden, we
Are linked as children in a circle dancing:
My Dear One is mine as mirrors are lonely,
And the high green hill sits always by the sea.

W. H. AUDEN

The Tempest (Act I, sc ii)

CALIBAN: I must eat my dinner.
This island's mine, by Sycorax my mother,
Which thou tak'st from me. When thou cam'st first,
Thou strok'st me and made much of me, wouldst give me
Water with berries in't, and teach me how
To name the bigger light, and how the less,
That burn by day and night; and then I lov'd thee,
And show'd thee all the qualities o' th' isle,
The fresh springs, brine-pits, barren place and fertile.
Curs'd be I that did so! All the charms
Of Sycorax, toads, beetles, bats, light on you!
For I am all the subjects that you have,
Which first was mine own king; . . .

WILLIAM SHAKESPEARE

Thrice Toss these Oaken Ashes in the Air

Thrice toss these oaken ashes in the air.
Thrice sit thou mute in this enchanted chair.
Then thrice three times tie up this true love's knot,
And murmur soft: She will, or she will not.

Go burn these poisonous weeds in yon blue fire,
These screech-owl's feathers and this prickling briar,
This cypress gathered at a dead man's grave,
That all thy fears and cares an end may have.

Then come, you fairies, dance with me a round;
Melt her hard heart with your melodious sound.
In vain are all the charms I can devise;
She hath an art to break them with her eyes.

THOMAS CAMPION

A Girl's Hair

He who could win the girl I love
would win a grove of light,
with her silken, starry hair
in golden columns from her head,
dragon fire lighting up a door,
three chains like the Milky Way.
She sets alight in one bush
a roof of hair like a bonfire.
Yellow broom or a great birch tree
is this gold-topped girl of Maelor.
A host coloured like angels,
her armour's many-branched,
a peacock-feather pennon,
a tall bush like the golden door,
all this lively looking hair
virtued like the sun, fetter of girls.
Anyone would know, were he a goldsmith,
who owns this fine strong hair.
In summer she has on her head
something like the Golden Hillside.
This fair growth is the girl's garment,
a tent for the sun, or harp strings,
ears of corn closed in above,
reed peelings as ornaments for the breast;
a peahen constantly carrying
hair of broom from head to ground,
a noose of woven amber,
the gold of corn like twig-chains;
her hair's a tree-high woodland,
a twig-crown of new wax.
Labour of bees has ripened
the seeds of warmth from a girl's flesh,
saffron on the herb eyebright,
cherries of gold, like the stars of night.
A good band round its coming growth,
fresh water-grass, golden water-hair,

lye water wets it like sweet herbs;
yellow-hammer head, bush of silk;
a sheaf of Mary Magdalen's broom
is the gold band that binds her hair.
If we let it down all glowing,
she'll wear a gown of golden hair.
It covers her two breasts
from its roof of gold in two fathoms,
fair ringlets, load of a girl's head,
flax before bush of yellow.
If spread out, the bush is gold:
was ever bush so yellow?
In order that from the christening font
the oil of faith should mark her head,
giving life to the sun's bush,
there's no such bush now under the sun.

DAFYDD AB EDMWND
TRANSLATED FROM THE WELSH
BY GWYN WILLIAMS

From Ovid's Banquet of Sense

In a loose robe of Tynsell foorth she came,
Nothing but it betwixt her nakednes
And envious light. The downward burning flame,
Of her rich hayre did threaten new accesse,
    Of ventrous *Phaeton* to scorch the fields:
And thus to bathing came our Poets Goddesse,
    Her handmaides bearing all things pleasure yeelds
To such a service; Odors most delighted,
And purest linnen which her lookes had whited.

45

Then cast she off her robe, and stood upright,
As lightning breakes out of a laboring cloude;
Or as the Morning heaven casts off the Night,
Or as that heaven cast off it selfe, and showde
  Heavens upper light, to which the brightest day
Is but a black and melancholy shroude:
  Or as when *Venus* striv'd her soveraine sway
Of charmfull beautie, in yong Troyes desire,
So stood *Corynna* vanishing her tire.

A soft enflowred banck embrac'd the founte;
Of *Chloris* ensignes, an abstracted field;
Where grew Melanthy, great in Bees account,
Amareus, that precious Balme dooth yeeld,
  Enameld Pansies, us'd at Nuptials still,
Dianas arrow, *Cupid's* crimson shielde,
  Ope-morne, night-shade, and *Venus* navill,
Solemne Violets, hanging head as shamed,
And verdant Calaminth, for odor famed;

Sacred Nepenthe, purgative of care,
And soveraine Rumex that doth rancor kill,
Sya, and Hyacinth, that Furies weare,
White and red Jessamines, Merry, Melliphill:
  Fayre Crowne-imperiall, Emperor of Flowers,
Immortall Amaranth, white Aphrodill,
  And cup-like Twillpants, stroude in *Bacchus* Bowres,
These cling about this Natures naked Jem,
To taste her sweetes, as Bees doe swarme on them.

And now she usde the Founte, where *Niobe*,
Toomb'd in her selfe, pourde her lost soule in teares,
Upon the bosome of this Romaine *Phoebe*;
Who, bathd and Odord, her bright lyms she rears,
  And drying her on that disparent rounde,
Her Lute she takes t'enamoure heavenly eares,
  And try if with her voyces vitall sounde,
She could warme life through those colde statues spread,
And cheere the Dame that wept when she was dead.

46

And thus she sung, all naked as she sat,
Laying the happy Lute upon her thigh,
Not thinking any neere to wonder at
The blisse of her sweete brests divinitie.

GEORGE CHAPMAN

Song

I feed a flame within which so torments me
That it both pains my heart, and yet contents me:
'Tis such a pleasing smart, and I so love it,
That I had rather die, then once remove it.

Yet he for whom I grieve shall never know it,
My tongue does not betray, nor my eyes show it:
Not a sigh nor a tear my pain discloses,
But they fall silently like dew on Roses.

Thus to prevent my love from being cruel,
My heart's the sacrifice as 'tis the fuel:
And while I suffer this to give him quiet,
My faith rewards my love, though he deny it.

On his eyes will I gaze, and there delight me;
While I conceal my love, no frown can fright me:
To be more happy I dare not aspire;
Nor can I fall more low, mounting no higher.

JOHN DRYDEN

Elegy 19 – To his Mistress Going to Bed

Come, Madam, come, all rest my powers defy,
Until I labour, I in labour lie.
The foe oft-times having the foe in sight,
Is tired with standing though they never fight.
Off with that girdle, like heaven's zone glistering,
But a far fairer world encompassing.
Unpin that spangled breastplate which you wear,
That th' eyes of busy fools may be stopped there.
Unlace yourself, for that harmonious chime
Tells me from you, that now 'tis your bed time.
Off with that happy busk, which I envy,
That still can be, and still can stand so nigh.
Your gown going off, such beauteous state reveals,
As when from flowery meads th' hill's shadow steals.
Off with that wiry coronet and show
The hairy diadem which on you doth grow;
Now off with those shoes, and then safely tread
In this love's hallowed temple, this soft bed.
In such white robes heaven's angels used to be
Received by men; thou angel bring'st with thee
A heaven like Mahomet's paradise; and though
Ill spirits walk in white, we easily know
By this these angels from an evil sprite,
Those set our hairs, but these our flesh upright.
    Licence my roving hands, and let them go
Before, behind, between, above, below.
O my America, my new found land,
My kingdom, safeliest when with one man manned,
My mine of precious stones, my empery,
How blessed am I in this discovering thee!
To enter in these bonds, is to be free;
Then where my hand is set, my seal shall be.
    Full nakedness, all joys are due to thee.
As souls unbodied, bodies unclothed must be,
To taste whole joys. Gems which you women use
Are like Atlanta's balls, cast in men's views,

48

That when a fool's eye lighteth on a gem,
His earthly soul may covet theirs, not them.
Like pictures, or like books' gay coverings made
For laymen, are all women thus arrayed;
Themselves are mystic books, which only we
Whom their imputed grace will dignify
Must see revealed. Then since I may know,
As liberally, as to a midwife, show
Thyself: cast all, yea, this white linen hence,
Here is no penance, much less innocence.
     To teach thee, I am naked first, when then
What needst thou have more covering than a man.

JOHN DONNE

A Rapture

I will enjoy thee now, my Celia, come,
And fly with me to Love's Elysium.
The giant, Honour, that keeps cowards out,
Is but a masquer, and the servile rout
Of baser subjects only bend in vain
To the vast idol; whilst the nobler train
Of valiant lovers daily sail between
The huge Colossus' legs, and pass unseen
Unto the blissful shore. Be bold and wise,
And we shall enter: the grim Swiss denies
Only to tame fools a passage, that not know
He is but form and only frights in show
The duller eyes that look from far; draw near
And thou shalt scorn what we were wont to fear.
We shall see how the stalking pageant goes
With borrow'd legs, a heavy load to those
That made and bear him; not, as we once thought,

The seed of gods, but a weak model wrought
By greedy men, that seek to enclose the common,
And within private arms empale free woman.
    Come, then, and mounted on the wings of Love
We'll cut the flitting air and soar above
The monster's head, and in the noblest seats
Of those blest shades quench and renew our heats.
There shall the queens of love and innocence,
Beauty and Nature, banish all offence
From our close ivy-twines; there I'll behold
Thy bared snow and thy unbraided gold;
There my enfranchised hand on every side
Shall o'er thy naked polish'd ivory slide.
No curtain there, though of transparent lawn,
Shall be before thy virgin-treasure drawn;
But the rich mine, to the enquiring eye
Exposed, shall ready still for mintage lie,
And we will coin young Cupids. There a bed
Of roses and fresh myrtles shall be spread,
Under the cooler shade of cypress groves;
Our pillows of the down of Venus' doves,
Whereon our panting limbs we'll gently lay,
In the faint respites of our active play:
That so our slumbers may in dreams have leisure
To tell the nimble fancy our past pleasure,
And so our souls, that cannot be embraced,
Shall the embraces of our bodies taste.
Meanwhile the bubbling stream shall court the shore,
Th' enamour'd chirping wood-choir shall adore
In varied tunes the deity of love;
The gentle blasts of western winds shall move
The trembling leaves, and through their close boughs
        breathe
Still music, whilst we rest ourselves beneath
Their dancing shade; till a soft murmur, sent
From souls entranced in amorous languishment,
Rouse us, and shoot into our veins fresh fire,
Till we in their sweet ecstasy expire.

Then, as the empty bee that lately bore
Into the common treasure all her store,
Flies 'bout the painted field with nimble wing,
Deflow'ring the fresh virgins of the spring,
So will I rifle all the sweets that dwell
In my delicious paradise, and swell
My bag with honey, drawn forth by the power
Of fervent kisses from each spicy flower.
I'll seize the rose-buds in their perfumed bed,
The violet knots, like curious mazes spread
O'er all the garden, taste the ripen'd cherry,
The warm firm apple, tipp'd with coral berry:
Then will I visit with a wand'ring kiss
The vale of lilies and the bower of bliss;
And where the beauteous region doth divide
Into two milky ways, my lips shall slide
Down those smooth alleys, wearing as they go
A tract for lovers on the printed snow;
Thence climbing o'er the swelling Apennine,
Retire into thy grove of eglantine,
Where I will all those ravish'd sweets distil
Through Love's alembic, and with chemic skill
From the mix'd mass one sovereign balm derive,
Then bring that great elixir to thy hive.
  Now in more subtle wreaths I will entwine
My sinewy thighs, my legs and arms with thine;
Thou like a sea of milk shalt lie display'd,
Whilst I the smooth calm ocean invade
With such a tempest, as when Jove of old
Fell down on Danaë in a storm of gold;
Yet my tall pine shall in the Cyprian strait
Ride safe at anchor and unlade her freight:
My rudder with thy bold hand, like a tried
And skilful pilot, thou shalt steer, and guide
My bark into love's channel, where it shall
Dance, as the bounding waves do rise or fall.
Then shall thy circling arms embrace and clip
My willing body, and thy balmy lip

Bathe me in juice of kisses, whose perfume
Like a religious incense shall consume,
And send up holy vapours to those powers
That bless our loves and crown our sportful hours,
That with such halcyon calmness fix our souls
In steadfast peace, as no affright controls.
There, no rude sounds shake us with sudden starts;
No jealous ears, when we unrip our hearts,
Suck our discourse in; no observing spies
This blush, that glance traduce; no envious eyes
Watch our close meetings; nor are we betray'd
To rivals by the bribed chambermaid.
No wedlock bonds unwreathe our twisted loves,
We seek no midnight arbour, no dark groves
To hide our kisses: there, the hated name
Of husband, wife, lust, modest, chaste or shame,
Are vain and empty words, whose very sound
Was never heard in the Elysian ground.
All things are lawful there, that may delight
Nature or unrestrained appetite;
Like and enjoy, to will and act is one:
We only sin when Love's rites are not done.
    The Roman Lucrece there reads the divine
Lectures of love's great master, Aretine,
And knows as well as Lais how to move
Her pliant body in the act of love;
To quench the burning ravisher she hurls
Her limbs into a thousand winding curls,
And studies artful postures, such as be
Carved on the bark of every neighbouring tree
By learned hands, that so adorn'd the rind
Of those fair plants, which, as they lay entwined,
Have fann'd their glowing fires. The Grecian dame,
That in her endless web toil'd for a name
As fruitless as her work, doth there display
Herself before the youth of Ithaca,
And th' amorous sport of gamesome nights prefer
Before dull dreams of the lost traveller.

Daphne hath broke her bark, and that swift foot
Which th' angry gods had fasten'd with a root
To the fix'd earth, doth now unfetter'd run
To meet th' embraces of the youthful Sun.
She hangs upon him like his Delphic lyre;
Her kisses blow the old, and breathe new fire;
Full of her god, she sings inspired lays,
Sweet odes of love, such as deserve the bays,
Which she herself was. Next her, Laura lies
In Petrarch's learned arms, drying those eyes
That did in such sweet smooth-paced numbers flow,
As made the world enamour'd of his woe.
These, and ten thousand beauties more, that died
Slave to the tyrant, now enlarged deride
His cancell'd laws, and for their time mis-spent
Pay into Love's exchequer double rent.
    Come then, my Celia, we'll no more forbear
To taste our joys, struck with a panic fear,
But will depose from his imperious sway
This proud usurper, and walk free as they,
With necks unyoked; nor is it just that he
Should fetter your soft sex with chastity,
Whom Nature made unapt for abstinence;
When yet this false impostor can dispense
With human justice and with sacred right,
And, maugre both their laws, command me fight
With rivals or with emulous loves that dare
Equal with thine their mistress' eyes or hair.
If thou complain of wrong, and call my sword
To carve out thy revenge, upon that word
He bids me fight and kill; or else he brands
With marks of infamy my coward hands.
And yet religion bids from blood-shed fly,
And damns me for that act. Then tell me why
    This goblin Honour, which the world adores,
    Should make men atheists, and not women whores?

53

A New Song

Sylvia the fair, in the bloom of Fifteen,
Felt an innocent warmth, as she lay on the green;
She had heard of a pleasure, and something she guest
By the towzing and tumbling and touching her Breast;
She saw the men eager, but was at a loss,
What they meant by their sighing, and kissing so close;
    By their praying and whining
    And clasping and twining,
    And panting and wishing,
    And sighing and kissing
    And sighing and kissing so close.

(II)

Ah she cry'd, ah for a languishing Maid
In a Country of Christians to die without aid!
Not a Whig, or a Tory, or Trimmer at least,
Or a Protestant Parson, or Catholick Priest,
To instruct a young Virgin, that is at a loss
What they meant by their sighing, and kissing so close!
    By their praying and whining
    And clasping and twining,
    And panting and wishing,
    And sighing and kissing
    And sighing and kissing so close.

Cupid in Shape of a Swayn did appear,
He saw the sad wound, and in pity drew near,
Then show'd her his Arrow, and bid her not fear,
For the pain was no more than a Maiden may bear;
When the balm was infus'd she was not at a loss,
What they meant by their sighing and kissing so close;
 By their praying and whining,
 And clasping and twining,
 And panting and wishing,
 And sighing and kissing,
 And sighing and kissing so close.

JOHN DRYDEN

My Thing is My Own

I a tender young Maid have been courted by many,
Of all sorts and Trades as ever was any:
A spruce Haberdasher first spake me fair,
But I would have nothing to do with Small ware.
 My Thing is my own, and I'll keep it so still,
 Yet other young Lasses may do what they will.

A sweet scented Courtier did give me a Kiss,
And promis'd me Mountains if I would be his,
But I'll not believe him, for it is too true,
Some Courtiers do promise much more than they do.
 My thing is my own, and I'll keep it so still,
 Yet other young Lasses may do what they will.

A fine Man of Law did come out of the Strand,
To plead his own Cause with his Fee in his Hand;
He made a brave Motion but that would not do,
For I did dismiss him, and Nonsuit him too.
 My thing is my own, and I'll keep it so still,
 Yet other young Lasses may do what they will.

Next came a young Fellow, a notable Spark,
(With Green Bag and Inkhorn, a Justices Clark)
He pull'd out his Warrant to make all appear,
But I sent him away with a Flea in his Ear.
   My thing is my own, and I'll keep it so still,
   Yet other young Lasses may do what they will.

A Master of Musick came with an intent,
To give me a Lesson on my Instrument,
I thank'd him for nothing, but bid him be gone,
For my little Fiddle should not be plaid on.
   My thing is my own, and I'll keep it so still,
   Yet other young Lasses may do what they will.

An Usurer came with abundance of Cash,
But I had no mind to come under his Lash,
He profer'd me Jewels, and great store of Gold,
But I would not Mortgage my little Free-hold.
   My thing is my own, and I'll keep it so still,
   Yet other young Lasses may do what they will.

A blunt Lieutenant surpriz'd my Placket,
And fiercely began to rifle and sack it,
I mustered my Spirits up and became bold,
And forc'd my Lieutenant to quit his strong hold.
   My thing is my own, and I'll keep it so still,
   Yet other young Lasses may do what they will.

A Crafty young Bumpkin that was very rich,
And us'd with his Bargains to go thro' stitch,
Did tender a Sum, but it would not avail,
That I should admit him my Tenant in tayl.
   My Thing is my own, and I'll keep it so still,
   Yet other young Lasses may do what they will.

A fine dapper Taylor, with a Yard in his Hand,
Did profer his Service to be at Command,
He talk'd of a slit I had above Knee,
But I'll have no Taylors to stitch it for me.
    My Thing is my own, and I'll keep it so still,
    Yet other young Lasses may do what they will.

A Gentleman that did talk much of his Grounds,
His Horses, his Setting-Dogs, and his Grey-hounds,
Put in for a Course, and us'd all his Art,
But he mist of the Sport, for Puss would not start,
    My Thing is my own, and I'll keep it so still,
    Yet other young Lasses may do what they will.

A pretty young Squire new come to the Town,
To empty his Pockets, and so to go down,
Did profer a kindness, but I would have none,
The same that he us'd to his Mother's Maid Joan.
    My Thing is my own, and I'll keep it so still,
    Yet other young Lasses may do what they will.

Now here I could reckon a hundred and more,
Besides all the Gamesters recited before,
That made their addresses in hopes of a snap
But as young as I was I understood Trap.
    My thing is my own, and I'll keep it so still,
    Until I be Marryed, say Men what they will.

ANON

Antony and Cleopatra (Act II, sc ii)

ENOBARBUS : When she first met Mark Antony she purs'd
up his heart, upon the river of Cydnus.

AGRIPPA : There she appear'd indeed! Or my reporter
devis'd well for her.

ENOBARBUS : I will tell you.
The barge she sat in, like a burnish'd throne,
Burn'd on the water. The poop was beaten gold;
Purple the sails, and so perfumed that
The winds were love-sick with them; the oars were silver,
Which to the tune of flutes kept stroke, and made
The water which they beat to follow faster,
As amorous of their strokes. For her own person,
It beggar'd all description. She did lie
In her pavilion, cloth-of-gold, of tissue,
O'erpicturing that Venus where we see
The fancy out-work nature. On each side her
Stood pretty dimpled boys, like smiling Cupids,
With divers-colour'd fans, whose wind did seem
To glow the delicate cheeks which they did cool,
And what they undid did.

AGRIPPA : O, rare for Antony!

ENOBARBUS : Her gentlewomen, like the Nereides,
So many mermaids, tended her i' th' eyes,
And made their bends adornings. At the helm
A seeming mermaid steers. The silken tackle
Swell with the touches of those flower-soft hands
That yarely frame the office. From the barge
A strange invisible perfume hits the sense
Of the adjacent wharfs. The city cast
Her people out upon her; and Antony,
Enthron'd i' th' market-place, did sit alone,
Whistling to th' air; which, but for vacancy,
Had gone to gaze on Cleopatra too,
And made a gap in nature.

AGRIPPA : Rare Egyptian!

ENOBARBUS : Upon her landing, Antony sent to her,

Invited her to supper. She replied
It should be better he became her guest;
Which she entreated. Our courteous Antony,
Whom ne'er the word of 'No' woman heard speak,
Being barber'd ten times o'er, goes to the feast,
And for his ordinary pays his heart
For what his eyes eat only.
AGRIPPA: Royal wench!
She made great Cæsar lay his sword to bed.
He ploughed her, and she cropp'd.
ENOBARBUS: I saw her once
Hop forty paces through the public street;
And, having lost her breath, she spoke, and panted,
That she did make defect perfection,
And, breathless, pow'r breathe forth.
MAECENAS: Now Antony must leave her utterly.
ENOBARBUS: Never! He will not.
Age cannot wither her, nor custom stale
Her infinite variety. Other women cloy
The appetites they feed, but she makes hungry
Where most she satisfies; for vilest things
Become themselves in her, that the holy priests
Bless her when she is riggish.

WILLIAM SHAKESPEARE

Elegy 16 – On his Mistress

By our first strange and fatal interview,
By all desires which thereof did ensue,
By our long starving hopes, by that remorse
Which my words' masculine persuasive force
Begot in thee, and by the memory
Of hurts, which spies and rivals threatened me,
I calmly beg: but by thy father's wrath,
By all pains, which want and divorcement hath,
I conjure thee; and all the oaths which I
And thou have sworn to seal joint constancy,
Here I unswear, and overswear them thus,
Thou shalt not love by ways so dangerous.
Temper, O fair love, love's impetuous rage,
Be my true mistress still, not my feigned page;
I'll go, and, by thy kind leave, leave behind
Thee, only worthy to nurse in my mind
Thirst to come back; oh, if thou die before,
From other lands my soul towards thee shall soar,
Thy (else almighty) beauty cannot move
Rage from the seas, nor thy love teach them love,
Nor tame wild Boreas' harshness; thou hast read
How roughly he in pieces shivered
Fair Orithea, whom he swore he loved.
Fall ill or good, 'tis madness to have proved
Dangers unurged; feed on this flattery,
That absent lovers one in th' other be.
Dissemble nothing, not a boy, nor change
Thy body's habit, nor mind's; be not strange
To thy self only; all will spy in thy face
A blushing womanly discovering grace;
Richly clothed apes, are called apes, and as soon
Eclipsed as bright we call the moon the moon.
Men of France, changeable chameleons,
Spitals of diseases, shops of fashions,
Love's fuellers, and the rightest company
Of players, which upon the world's stage be,

Will quickly know thee, and know thee; and alas
Th' indifferent Italian, as we pass
His warm land, well content to think thee page,
Will hunt thee with such lust, and hideous rage,
As Lot's fair guests were vexed. But none of these
Nor spongy hydroptic Dutch shall thee displease,
If thou stay here. Oh stay here, for, for thee
England is only a worthy gallery,
To walk in expectation, till from thence
Our greatest King call thee to his presence.
When I am gone, dream me some happiness,
Nor let thy looks our long-hid love confess,
Nor praise, nor dispraise me, nor bless nor curse
Openly love's force, nor in bed fright thy nurse
With midnight's startings, crying out, 'Oh, oh
Nurse, O my love is slain, I saw him go
O'er the white Alps alone; I saw him, I,
Assailed, fight, taken, stabbed, bleed, fall, and die.'
Augur me better chance, except dread Jove
Think it enough for me to have had thy love.

JOHN DONNE

Memory

One had a lovely face,
And two or three had charm,
But charm and face were in vain
Because the mountain grass
Cannot but keep the form
Where the mountain hare has lain.

W. B. YEATS

The force that through the green fuse drives the flower

The force that through the green fuse drives the flower
Drives my green age; that blasts the roots of trees
Is my destroyer.
And I am dumb to tell the crooked rose
My youth is bent by the same wintry fever.

The force that drives the water through the rocks
Drives my red blood; that dries the mouthing streams
Turns mine to wax.
And I am dumb to mouth unto my veins
How at the mountain spring the same mouth sucks.

The hand that whirls the water in the pool
Stirs the quicksand; that ropes the blowing wind
Hauls my shroud sail.
And I am dumb to tell the hanging man
How of my clay is made the hangman's lime.

The lips of time leech to the fountain head;
Love drips and gathers, but the fallen blood
Shall calm her sores.
And I am dumb to tell a weather's wind
How time has ticked a heaven round the stars.

And I am dumb to tell the lover's tomb
How at my sheet goes the same crooked worm.

DYLAN THOMAS

Sonnet CXLVII

My love is as a fever, longing still
For that which longer nurseth the disease;
Feeding on that which doth preserve the ill,
The uncertain sickly appetite to please.
My reason, the physician to my love,
Angry that his prescriptions are not kept,
Hath left me, and I desperate now approve
Desire is death, which physic did except.
Past cure I am, now Reason is past care,
And frantic-mad with evermore unrest;
My thoughts and my discourse as madmen's are,
At random from the truth vainly express'd;
 For I have sworn thee fair, and thought thee bright,
 Who art as black as hell, as dark as night.

WILLIAM SHAKESPEARE

The Flea

Mark but this flea, and mark in this,
How little that which thou deny'st me is;
Me it sucked first, and now sucks thee,
And in this flea, our two bloods mingled be;
Confess it, this cannot be said
A sin, or shame, or loss of maidenhead,
 Yet this enjoys before it woo,
 And pampered swells with one blood made of two,
 And this, alas, is more than we would do.

Oh stay, three lives in one flea spare,
Where we almost, nay more than married are.
This flea is you and I, and this
Our marriage bed, and marriage temple is;
Though parents grudge, and you, we'are met,
And cloistered in these living walls of jet.
    Though use make you apt to kill me,
    Let not to this, self murder added be,
    And sacrilege, three sins in killing three.

Cruel and sudden, hast thou since
Purpled thy nail, in blood of innocence?
In what could this flea guilty be,
Except in that drop which it sucked from thee?
Yet thou triumph'st, and say'st that thou
Find'st not thyself, nor me the weaker now;
    'Tis true, then learn how false, fears be;
    Just so much honour, when thou yield'st to me,
    Will waste, as this flea's death took life from thee.

JOHN DONNE

Inordinate Love

I shall say what inordinat love is:
The furiosite and wodness of minde,
A instinguible brenning fawting blis,
A gret hungre, insaciat to finde,
A dowcet ille, a ivell swetness blinde,
A right wonderfulle, sugred, swete errour,
Withoute labour rest, contrary to kinde,
Or withoute quiete to have huge labour.

ANON

Merciles Beaute

A Triple Roundel

Your yen two wol slee me sodenly;
I may the beautee of hem not sustene,
So woundeth hit thourghout my herte kene.

And but your word wol helen hastily
My hertes wounde, while that hit is grene,
   Your yen two wol slee me sodenly;
   I may the beautee of hem not sustene.

Upon my trouthe I sey you feithfully
That ye ben of my lyf and deeth the quene;
For with my deeth the trouthe shal be sene.
   Your yen two wol slee me sodenly;
   I may the beautee of hem not sustene,
   So woundeth it thourghout my herte kene.

(II)

So hath your beautee fro your herte chaced
Pitee, that me ne availeth not to pleyne;
For Daunger halt your mercy in his cheyne.

Giltles my deeth thus han ye me purchaced;
I sey you sooth, me nedeth not to feyne;
   So hath your beautee fro your herte chaced
   Pitee, that me ne availeth not to pleyne.

Allas! that Nature hath in you compassed
So greet beautee, that no man may atteyne
To mercy, though he sterve for the peyne.
   So hath your beautee fro your herte chaced
   Pitee, that me ne availeth not to pleyne;
   For Daunger halt your mercy in his cheyne.

Sin I fro Love escaped am so fat,
I never thenk to ben in his prison lene;
Sin I am free, I counte him not a bene.

He may answere, and seye this and that;
I do no fors, I speke right as I mene.
  Sin I fro Love escaped am so fat,
  I never thenk to ben in his prison lene.

Love hath my name ystrike out of his sclat,
And he is strike out of my bokes clene
For evermo; [ther] is non other mene.
  Sin I fro Love escaped am so fat,
  I never thenk to ben in his prison lene;
  Sin I am free, I counte him not a bene.

Explicit.

GEOFFREY CHAUCER

The Good Morrow

I wonder by my troth, what thou, and I
    Did, till we loved? were we not weaned till then,
But sucked on country pleasures, childishly?
    Or snorted we in the seven sleepers' den?
'Twas so; but this, all pleasures fancies be.
If ever any beauty I did see,
Which I desired, and got, 'twas but a dream of thee.

And now good morrow to our waking souls,
    Which watch not one another out of fear;
For love, all love of other sights controls,
    And makes one little room, an every where.
Let sea-discoverers to new worlds have gone,
Let maps to others, worlds on worlds have shown,
Let us possess one world, each hath one, and is one.

66

My face in thine eye, thine in mine appears,
  And true plain hearts do in the faces rest,
Where can we find two better hemispheres
  Without sharp north, without declining west?
What ever dies, was not mixed equally;
  If our two loves be one, or, thou and I
Love so alike, that none do slacken, none can die.

JOHN DONNE

Oh Wert Thou in the Cauld Blast

Oh wert thou in the cauld blast,
    On yonder lea, on yonder lea;
My plaidie to the angry airt,
    I'd shelter thee, I'd shelter thee:
Or did misfortune's bitter storms
    Around thee blaw, around thee blaw,
Thy bield should be my bosom,
    To share it a', to share it a'.

Or were I in the wildest waste,
    Sae black and bare, sae black and bare,
The desart were a paradise,
    If thou wert there, if thou wert there.
Or were I monarch o' the globe,
    Wi' thee to reign, wi' thee to reign;
The brightest jewel in my crown,
    Wad be my queen, wad be my queen.

ROBERT BURNS

The Love Song of J. Alfred Prufrock

S'io credessi che mia risposta fosse
a persona che mai tornasse al mondo,
questa fiamma staria senza più scosse.
Ma per ciò che giammai di questo fondo
non tornò vivo alcun, s' i' odo il vero,
senza tema d'infamia ti rispondo.

Let us go then, you and I,
When the evening is spread out against the sky
Like a patient etherised upon a table;
Let us go, through certain half-deserted streets,
The muttering retreats
Of restless nights in one-night cheap hotels
And sawdust restaurants with oyster-shells:
Streets that follow like a tedious argument
Of insidious intent
To lead you to an overwhelming question . . .
Oh, do not ask, 'What is it?'
Let us go and make our visit.

In the room the women come and go
Talking of Michelangelo.

The yellow fog that rubs its back upon the window-panes,
The yellow smoke that rubs its muzzle on the window-panes,
Licked its tongue into the corners of the evening,
Lingered upon the pools that stand in drains,
Let fall upon its back the soot that falls from chimneys,
Slipped by the terrace, made a sudden leap,
And seeing that it was a soft October night,
Curled once about the house, and fell asleep.

And indeed there will be time
For the yellow smoke that slides along the street
Rubbing its back upon the window-panes;
There will be time, there will be time
To prepare a face to meet the faces that you meet;
There will be time to murder and create,
And time for all the works and days of hands
That lift and drop a question on your plate;
Time for you and time for me,
And time yet for a hundred indecisions,
And for a hundred visions and revisions,
Before the taking of a toast and tea.

   In the room the women come and go
Talking of Michelangelo.

   And indeed there will be time
To wonder, 'Do I dare?' and, 'Do I dare?'
Time to turn back and descend the stair,
With a bald spot in the middle of my hair—
(They will say: 'How his hair is growing thin!')
My morning coat, my collar mounting firmly to the chin,
My necktie rich and modest, but asserted by a simple pin—
(They will say: 'But how his arms and legs are thin!')
Do I dare
Disturb the universe?
In a minute there is time
For decisions and revisions which a minute will reverse.

   For I have known them all already, known them all—
Have known the evenings, mornings, afternoons,
I have measured out my life with coffee spoons;
I know the voices dying with a dying fall
Beneath the music from a farther room.
   So how should I presume?

And I have known the eyes already, known them all—
The eyes that fix you in a formulated phrase,
And when I am formulated, sprawling on a pin,
When I am pinned and wriggling on the wall,
Then how should I begin
To spit out all the butt-ends of my days and ways?
   And how should I presume?

And I have known the arms already, known them all—
Arms that are braceleted and white and bare
(But in the lamplight, downed with light brown hair!)
Is it perfume from a dress
That makes me so digress?
Arms that lie along a table, or wrap about a shawl.
   And should I then presume?
   And how should I begin?

          .   .   .   .   .

Shall I say, I have gone at dusk through narrow streets
And watched the smoke that rises from the pipes
Of lonely men in shirt-sleeves, leaning out of windows? . .

I should have been a pair of ragged claws
Scuttling across the floors of silent seas.

          .   .   .   .   .

And the afternoon, the evening, sleeps so peacefully!
Smoothed by long fingers,
Asleep . . . tired . . . or it malingers,
Stretched on the floor, here beside you and me.
Should I, after tea and cakes and ices,
Have the strength to force the moment to its crisis?
But though I have wept and fasted, wept and prayed,
Though I have seen my head (grown slightly bald)
          brought in upon a platter,
I am no prophet—and here's no great matter;
I have seen the moment of my greatness flicker,
And I have seen the eternal Footman hold my coat, and
          snicker,
And in short, I was afraid.

And would it have been worth it, after all,
After the cups, the marmalade, the tea,
Among the porcelain, among some talk of you and me,
Would it have been worth while,
To have bitten off the matter with a smile,
To have squeezed the universe into a ball
To roll it towards some overwhelming question,
To say: 'I am Lazarus, come from the dead,
Come back to tell you all, I shall tell you all'—
If one, settling a pillow by her head,
   Should say: 'That is not what I meant at all.
   That is not it, at all.'

And would it have been worth it, after all,
Would it have been worth while,
After the sunsets and the dooryards and the sprinkled streets,
After the novels, after the teacups, after the skirts that trail
   along the floor—
And this, and so much more?—
It is impossible to say just what I mean!
But as if a magic lantern threw the nerves in patterns on a
   screen:
Would it have been worth while
If one, settling a pillow or throwing off a shawl,
And turning toward the window, should say:
   'That is not it at all,
   That is not what I meant, at all.'

      . . . . .

No! I am not Prince Hamlet, nor was meant to be;
Am an attendant lord, one that will do
To swell a progress, start a scene or two,
Advise the prince; no doubt, an easy tool,
Deferential, glad to be of use,
Politic, cautious, and meticulous;
Full of high sentence, but a bit obtuse;
At times, indeed, almost ridiculous—
Almost, at times, the Fool.

I grow old . . . I grow old . . .
I shall wear the bottoms of my trousers rolled.

Shall I part my hair behind? Do I dare to eat a peach?
I shall wear white flannel trousers, and walk upon the beach.
I have heard the mermaids singing, each to each.

I do not think that they will sing to me.

I have seen them riding seaward on the waves
Combing the white hair of the waves blown back
When the wind blows the water white and black.

We have lingered in the chambers of the sea
By sea-girls wreathed with seaweed red and brown
Till human voices wake us, and we drown.

T. S. ELIOT

Song

Love still has something of the Sea,
    From whence his Mother rose;
No time his Slaves from Doubt can free,
    Nor give their Thoughts repose:

They are becalm'd in clearest Days,
    And in rough Weather tost;
They wither under cold Delays,
    Or are in Tempests lost.

One while they seem to touch the Port,
    Then straight into the Main,
Some angry Wind in cruel sport
    Their Vessel drives again.

At first, Disdain and Pride they fear,
    Which if they chance to scape,
Rivals and Falshood soon appear
    In a more dreadful shape.

By such Degrees to Joy they come,
    And are so long withstood,
So slowly they receive the Sum,
    It hardly does them good.

'Tis cruel to prolong a Pain,
    And to defer a Joy,
Believe me, gentle *Celemene*,
    Offends the winged Boy.

An hundred thousand Oaths your Fears
    Perhaps would not remove;
And if I gaz'd a hundred Years
    I could no deeper love.

SIR CHARLES SEDLEY

Chanson en *Si*

Si j'étais noble Faucon,
Tournoirais sur ton balcon . . .
— Taureau: foncerais ta porte . . .
— Vampire: te boirais morte . . .
        Te boirais!

— Geôlier: lèverais l'écrou . . .
— Rat: ferais un petit trou . . .
Si j'étais brise alizée,
Te mouillerais de rosée . . .
        Roserais!

Si j'étais gros Confesseur,
Te fouaillerais, ô ma Sœur!
Pour seconde pénitence,
Te dirais ce que je pense . . .
        Te dirais . . .

Si j'étais un maigre Apôtre,
Dirais: "Donnez-vous l'un l'autre,
Pour votre faim apaiser:
Le pain d'amour: Un baiser."
   Si j'étais!...

Si j'étais Frère-quêteur,
Quêterais ton petit cœur
Pour Dieu le Fils et le Père,
L'Eglise leur Sainte Mère...
   Quêterais!

Si j'étais Madone riche,
Jetterais bien, de ma niche,
Un regard, un sou béni
Pour le cantique fini...
   Jetterais!

Si j'étais un vieux bedeau,
Mettrais un cierge au rideau...
D'un goupillon d'eau bénite,
L'éteindrais, la vespre dite.
   L'éteindrais!

Si j'étais roide pendu,
Au ciel serais tout rendu:
Grimperais après ma corde,
Ancre de miséricorde,
   Grimperais!

Si j'étais femme... Eh, la Belle,
Tu ferais ma Colombelle...
A la porte les galants
Pourraient se percer les flancs...
   Te ferais...

Enfant, si j'étais la duègne
Rossinante qui te peigne,
Señora, si j'étais Toi . . .
J'ouvrirais au pauvre Moi.
        — Ouvrirais! —

TRISTAN CORBIÈRE

Balade

Hyd, Absolon, thy gilte tresses clere;
Ester, ley thou thy meknesse al adown;
Hyd, Jonathas, al thy frendly manere;
Penalopee and Marcia Catoun,
Make of youre wifhod no comparysoun;
Hyde ye youre beautes, Ysoude and Eleyne:
My lady cometh, that al this may disteyne.

Thy faire body, lat yt nat appere,
Lavyne; and thou, Lucresse of Rome toun,
And Polixene, that boghten love so dere,
And Cleopatre, with al thy passyoun,
Hyde ye your trouthe of love and your renoun;
And thou, Tisbe, that hast for love swich peyne:
My lady cometh, that al this may disteyne.

Herro, Dido, Laudomia, alle yfere,
And Phillis, hangyng for thy Demophoun,
And Canace, espied by thy chere,
Ysiphile, betrayed with Jasoun,
Maketh of your trouthe neythir boost ne soun;
Nor Ypermystre or Adriane, ye tweyne:
My lady cometh, that al this may dysteyne.

GEOFFREY CHAUCER

Sonnet CXXX

My mistress' eyes are nothing like the sun;
Coral is far more red than her lips' red:
If snow be white, why then her breasts are dun;
If hairs be wires, black wires grow on her head.
I have seen roses damask'd, red and white,
But no such roses see I in her cheeks;
And in some perfumes is there more delight
Than in the breath that from my mistress reeks.
I love to hear her speak, yet well I know
That music hath a far more pleasing sound:
I grant I never saw a goddess go,—
My mistress, when she walks, treads on the ground:
    And yet, by heaven, I think my love as rare
    As any she belied with false compare.

WILLIAM SHAKESPEARE

The Tryst

O luely, luely, cam she in
And luely she lay doun:
I kent her be her caller lips
And her breists sae sma' and roun'.

A' thru the nicht we spak nae word
Nor sinder'd bane frae bane:
A' thru the nicht I heard her hert
Gang soundin' wi' my ain.

76

It was about the waukrife hour
Whan cocks begin to craw
That she smool'd saftly thru the mirk
Afore the day wud daw.

Sae luely, luely, cam she in
Sae luely was she gaen;
And wi' her a' my simmer days
Like they had never been.

WILLIAM SOUTAR

From The Princess

'Now sleeps the crimson petal, now the white;
Nor waves the cypress in the palace walk;
Nor winks the gold fin in the porphyry font:
The fire-fly wakens: waken thou with me.

Now droops the milkwhite peacock like a ghost,
And like a ghost she glimmers on to me.

Now lies the Earth all Danaë to the stars,
And all thy heart lies open unto me.

Now slides the silent meteor on, and leaves
A shining furrow, as thy thoughts in me.

Now folds the lily all her sweetness up,
And slips into the bosom of the lake:
So fold thyself, my dearest, thou, and slip
Into my bosom and be lost in me.'

ALFRED, LORD TENNYSON

Sonnet LXXV

So are you to my thoughts as food to life,
Or as sweet-season'd showers are to the ground;
And for the peace of you I hold such strife
As 'twixt a miser and his wealth is found;
Now proud as an enjoyer, and anon
Doubting the filching age will steal his treasure;
Now counting best to be with you alone,
Then better'd that the world may see my pleasure:
Sometime all full with feasting on your sight,
And by and by clean starved for a look;
Possessing or pursuing no delight,
Save what is had or must from you be took.
   Thus do I pine and surfeit day by day,
   Or gluttoning on all, or all away.

WILLIAM SHAKESPEARE

Fra Bank to Bank

Fra bank to bank, fra wood to wood I rin,
   Ourhailit with my feeble fantasie;
   Like til a leaf that fallis from a tree,
Or til a reed ourblawin with the win.

Twa gods guides me: the ane of tham is blin,
   Yea and a bairn brocht up in vanitie;
   The next a wife ingenrit of the sea,
And lichter nor a dauphin with her fin.

Unhappy is the man for evermair
   That tills the sand and sawis in the air;
   But twice unhappier is he, I lairn,
That feidis in his hairt a mad desire,
And follows on a woman throw the fire,
   Led by a blind and teachit by a bairn.

MARK ALEXANDER BOYD

Antony and Cleopatra (Act IV, sc xiv)

ANTONY: Eros, thou yet behold'st me?
EROS: Ay, noble lord.
ANTONY: Sometime we see a cloud that's dragonish;
A vapour sometime like a bear or lion,
A tower'd citadel, a pendent rock,
A forked mountain, or blue promontory
With trees upon't that nod unto the world
And mock our eyes with air. Thou hast seen these signs;
They are black vesper's pageants.
EROS: Ay, my lord.
ANTONY: That which is now a horse, even with a thought
The rack dislimns, and makes it indistinct,
As water is in water.
EROS: It does, my lord.
ANTONY: My good knave Eros, now thy captain is
Even such a body. Here I am Antony;
Yet cannot hold this visible shape, my knave.
I made these wars for Egypt; and the Queen—
Whose heart I thought I had, for she had mine,
Which, whilst it was mine, had annex'd unto't
A million moe, now lost—she, Eros, has
Pack'd cards with Cæsar, and false-play'd my glory
Unto an enemy's triumph.
Nay, weep not, gentle Eros; there is left us
Ourselves to end ourselves.

WILLIAM SHAKESPEARE

A Nocturnal upon S. Lucy's Day,
being the shortest day

'Tis the year's midnight, and it is the day's,
Lucy's, who scarce seven hours herself unmasks,
   The sun is spent, and now his flasks
   Send forth light squibs, no constant rays;
     The world's whole sap is sunk:
The general balm th' hydroptic earth hath drunk,
Whither, as to the bed's-feet, life is shrunk,
Dead and interred; yet all these seem to laugh,
Compared with me, who am their epitaph.

Study me then, you who shall lovers be
At the next world, that is, at the next spring:
   For I am every dead thing,
   In whom love wrought new alchemy.
     For his art did express
A quintessence even from nothingness,
From dull privations, and lean emptiness
He ruined me, and I am re-begot
Of absence, darkness, death; things which are not.

All others, from all things, draw all that's good,
Life, soul, form, spirit, whence they being have;
   I, by love's limbeck, am the grave
   Of all, that's nothing. Oft a flood
     Have we two wept, and so
Drowned the whole world, us two; oft did we grow
To be two chaoses, when we did show
Care to aught else; and often absences
Withdrew our souls, and made us carcases.

But I am by her death (which word wrongs her)
Of the first nothing, the elixir grown;
   Were I a man, that I were one,
    I needs must know; I should prefer,
      If I were any beast,
Some ends, some means; yea plants, yea stones detest,
And love; all, all some properties invest;
If I an ordinary nothing were,
As shadow, a light, and body must be here.

But I am none; nor will my sun renew.
You lovers, for whose sake, the lesser sun
   At this time to the Goat is run
    To fetch new lust, and give it you,
        Enjoy your summer all;
Since she enjoys her long night's festival,
Let me prepare towards her, and let me call
This hour her vigil, and her eve, since this
Both the year's, and the day's deep midnight is.

JOHN DONNE

Sonnet CLI

Love is too young to know what conscience is;
Yet who knows not conscience is born of love?
Then, gentle cheater, urge not my amiss,
Lest guilty of my faults thy sweet self prove:
For, thou betraying me, I do betray
My nobler part to my gross body's treason;
My soul doth tell my body that he may
Triumph in love; flesh stays no farther reason,
But rising at thy name doth point out thee
As his triumphant prize. Proud of this pride,
He is contented thy poor drudge to be,
To stand in thy affairs, fall by thy side.
    No want of conscience hold it that I call
    Her 'love' for whose dear love I rise and fall.

WILLIAM SHAKESPEARE

Votaries of Both Sexes Cry First to Venus

Crying for pleasure,
Crying for pain,
Longing to see you
Again and again.

To the tune: Angels of Jesus, Angels of light, Singing to welcome The pilgrims of the night.
Hymns Ancient and Modern

But one stood up and said: I love
The love that comes in the dark fields,
In the late night, in the hot breathless dark night;
In the moony forest, when there is a moon,
In the moony rides of the dark forest.
I love this love; it is eerie if there is not

82

My love in *my* arms then. It is an excitement
In the arms of a person. It is exciting then,
It is such an excitement as is on the approach
Of Death; it is *my* love in *my* arms, and then
The trees and the dark trees and the soft grass and the
       moon
Are not arrogant, as they are if I am alone,
Not a measure, a great measure of indifference, not arrogant
Or in their way exciting either in a way that is too much.
Here this person standing up before Venus wept
And wept, and the tears of this person were warm
And this person then said: There is no love in my arms
No sweet person I love in my arms, and the tears
And the soft strong feelings I parade underneath the trees,
I lay them down; on the soft dark grass I lay down
My strong feelings. They are for you to eat up, Venus,
But you do not care for them much. Then they are
For the god who created me. Let him have them.

Then this person began to laugh and to dance
And Venus was offended; but behind Venus there came
First a little light, then some laughter, then a hand
That took up the great feelings, and then a blessing fell
Like the moon, and there was not any Venus any longer
But the votaries were not abashed, they were blessed

          Crying for pleasure,   *(tune as above)*
          Crying for pain,
          Longing to see you
          Again and again.

Yes this time when they sang their song they were blessed.

STEVIE SMITH

Sonnet CXLI

In faith, I do not love thee with mine eyes,
For they in thee a thousand errors note;
But 'tis my heart that loves what they despise,
Who, in despite of view, is pleas'd to dote.
Nor are mine ears with thy tongue's tune delighted;
Nor tender feeling, to base touches prone,
Nor taste, nor smell, desire to be invited
To any sensual feast with thee alone:
But my five wits nor my five senses can
Dissuade one foolish heart from serving thee,
Who leaves unsway'd the likeness of a man,
Thy proud heart's slave and vassal wretch to be:
    Only my plague thus far I count my gain,
    That she that makes me sin awards me pain.

WILLIAM SHAKESPEARE

A Deep-Sworn Vow

Others because you did not keep
That deep-sworn vow have been friends of mine;
Yet always when I look death in the face,
When I clamber to the heights of sleep,
Or when I grow excited with wine,
Suddenly I meet your face.

W. B. YEATS

Lament for Pasiphaë

Dying sun, shine warm a little longer!
My eye, dazzled with tears, shall dazzle yours,
Conjuring you to shine and not to move.
You, sun, and I all afternoon have laboured
Beneath a dewless and oppressive cloud –
A fleece now gilded with our common grief
That this must be a night without a moon.
Dying sun, shine warm a little longer!

Faithless she was not: she was very woman,
Smiling with dire impartiality,
Sovereign, with heart unmatched, adored of men,
Until Spring's cuckoo with bedraggled plumes
Tempted her pity and her truth betrayed.
Then she who shone for all resigned her being,
And this must be a night without a moon.
Dying sun, shine warm a little longer!

ROBERT GRAVES

Sonnet XXIX

When in disgrace with fortune and men's eyes
I all alone beweep my outcast state,
And trouble deaf heaven with my bootless cries,
And look upon myself, and curse my fate,
Wishing me like to one more rich in hope,
Featur'd like him, like him with friends possess'd,

Desiring this man's art, and that man's scope,
With what I most enjoy contented least;
Yet in these thoughts myself almost despising,
Haply I think on thee,—and then my state,
Like to the lark at break of day arising
From sullen earth, sings hymns at heaven's gate;
    For thy sweet love remember'd such wealth brings
    That then I scorn to change my state with kings.

WILLIAM SHAKESPEARE

In Memoriam

(XXVII)

I envy not in any moods
   The captive void of noble rage,
   The linnet born within the cage,
That never knew the summer woods:

I envy not the beast that takes
   His license in the field of time,
   Unfettered by the sense of crime,
To whom a conscience never wakes;

Nor, what may count itself as blest,
   The heart that never plighted troth
   But stagnates in the weeds of sloth;
Nor any want-begotten rest.

I hold it true, whate'er befall;
   I feel it, when I sorrow most;
   'Tis better to have loved and lost
Than never to have loved at all.

ALFRED, LORD TENNYSON

I Died for Beauty

I died for Beauty – but was scarce
Adjusted in the Tomb
When One who died for Truth, was lain
In an adjoining Room –

He questioned softly "Why I failed"?
"For Beauty", I replied –
"And I – for Truth – Themself are One –
We Brethren, are", He said –

86

And so, as Kinsmen, met a Night –
We talked between the Rooms –
Until the Moss had reached our lips –
And covered up – our names –

EMILY DICKINSON

No Road

Since we agreed to let the road between us
Fall to disuse,
And bricked our gates up, planted trees to screen us,
And turned all time's eroding agents loose,
Silence, and space, and strangers—our neglect
Has not had much effect.

Leaves drift unswept, perhaps; grass creeps unmown;
No other change.
So clear it stands, so little overgrown,
Walking that way tonight would not seem strange,
And still would be allowed. A little longer,
And time will be the stronger,

Drafting a world where no such road will run
From you to me;
To watch that world come up like a cold sun,
Rewarding others, is my liberty.
Not to prevent it is my will's fulfilment.
Willing it, my ailment.

PHILIP LARKIN

The Definition of Love

1

My Love is of a birth as rare
As 'tis for object strange and high:
It was begotten by despair
Upon Impossibility.

2

Magnanimous Despair alone
Could show me so divine a thing,
Where feeble Hope could ne'r have flown
But vainly flapt its Tinsel Wing.

3

And yet I quickly might arrive
Where my extended Soul is fixt,
But Fate does Iron wedges drive,
And alwaies crouds it self betwixt.

4

For Fate with jealous Eye does see
Two perfect Loves; nor lets them close:
Their union would her ruine be,
And her Tyrannick pow'r depose.

5

And therefore her Decrees of Steel
Us as the distant Poles have plac'd,
(Though Loves whole World on us doth wheel)
Not by themselves to be embrac'd.

6

Unless the giddy Heaven fall,
And Earth some new Convulsion tear;
And, us to joyn, the World should all
Be cramp'd into a *Planisphere*.

7

As Lines so Loves *oblique* may well
Themselves in every Angle greet:
But ours so truly *Paralel*,
Though infinite can never meet.

8

Therefore the Love which us doth bind.
But Fate so enviously debarrs,
Is the Conjunction of the Mind,
And Opposition of the Stars.

ANDREW MARVELL

I Cannot Live with You

I cannot live with You –
It would be Life –
And Life is over there –
Behind the Shelf

The Sexton keeps the Key to –
Putting up
Our Life – His Porcelain –
Like a Cup –

Discarded of the Housewife –
Quaint – or Broke –
A newer Sevres pleases –
Old Ones crack –

I could not die – with You –
For One must wait
To shut the Other's Gaze down –
You – could not –

And I – Could I stand by
And see You – freeze –
Without my Right of Frost –
Death's privilege?

Nor could I rise – with You –
Because Your Face
Would put out Jesus' –
That New Grace

Glow plain – and foreign
On my homesick Eye –
Except that You than He
Shone closer by –

They'd judge Us – How –
For You – served Heaven – You know,
Or sought to –
I could not –

Because You saturated Sight –
And I had no more Eyes
For sordid excellence
As Paradise

And were You lost, I would be –
Though My Name
Rang loudest
On the Heavenly fame –

And were You – saved –
And I – condemned to be
Where You were not –
That self – were Hell to Me –

So We must meet apart –
You there – I – here –
With just the Door ajar
That Oceans are – and Prayer –
And that White Sustenance –
Despair –

EMILY DICKINSON

Sonnet XIX

Devouring Time, blunt thou the lion's paws,
And make the earth devour her own sweet brood;
Pluck the keen teeth from the fierce tiger's jaws,
And burn the long-liv'd phœnix in her blood;
Make glad and sorry seasons as thou fleets,
And do whate'er thou wilt, swift-footed Time,
To the wide world and all her fading sweets;
But I forbid thee one most heinous crime:
O! carve not with thy hours my love's fair brow,
Nor draw no lines there with thine antique pen;
Him in thy course untainted do allow
For beauty's pattern to succeeding men.
    Yet, do thy worst, old Time: despite thy wrong,
    My love shall in my verse ever live young.

WILLIAM SHAKESPEARE

LIV

L'Irréparable

Pouvons-nous étouffer le vieux, le long Remords,
    Qui vit, s'agite et se tortille,
Et se nourrit de nous comme le ver des morts,
    Comme du chêne la chenille?
Pouvons-nous étouffer l'implacable Remords?

Dans quel philtre, dans quel vin, dans quelle tisane,
    Noierons-nous ce vieil ennemi,
Destructeur et gourmand comme la courtisane,
    Patient comme la fourmi?
Dans quel philtre? — dans quel vin? — dans quelle tisane?

Dis-le, belle sorcière, oh! dis, si tu le sais,
        A cet esprit comblé d'angoisse
Et pareil au mourant qu'écrasent les blessés,
        Que le sabot du cheval froisse,
Dis-le, belle sorcière, oh! dis, si tu le sais,

A cet agonisant que le loup déjà flaire
        Et que surveille le corbeau,
A ce soldat brisé! s'il faut qu'il désespère
        D'avoir sa croix et son tombeau;
Ce pauvre agonisant que déjà le loup flaire!

Peut-on illuminer un ciel bourbeux et noir?
        Peut-on déchirer des ténèbres
Plus denses que la poix, sans matin et sans soir,
        Sans astres, sans éclairs funèbres?
Peut-on illuminer un ciel bourbeux et noir?

L'Espérance qui brille aux carreaux de l'Auberge
        Est soufflée, est morte à jamais!
Sans lune et sans rayons, trouver où l'on héberge
        Les martyrs d'un chemin mauvais!
Le Diable a tout éteint aux carreaux de l'Auberge!

Adorable sorcière, aimes-tu les damnés?
        Dis, connais-tu l'irrémissible?
Connais-tu le Remords, aux traits empoisonnés,
        A qui notre cœur sert de cible?
Adorable sorcière, aimes-tu les damnés?

L'Irréparable ronge, avec sa dent maudite
        Notre âme, piteux monument,
Et souvent il attaque, ainsi que le termite,
        Par la base le bâtiment.
L'Irréparable ronge avec sa dent maudite!

— J'ai vu parfois, au fond d'un théâtre banal
    Qu'enflammait l'orchestre sonore,
Une fée allumer dans un ciel infernal
    Une miraculeuse aurore;
J'ai vu parfois au fond d'un théâtre banal

Un être, qui n'était que lumière, or et gaze,
    Terrasser l'énorme Satan;
Mais mon cœur, que jamais ne visite l'extase,
    Est un théâtre où l'on attend
Toujours, toujours en vain, l'Etre aux ailes de gaze!

CHARLES BAUDELAIRE

Sonnet XC

Then hate me when thou wilt; if ever, now;
Now, while the world is bent my deeds to cross,
Join with the spite of fortune, make me bow,
And do not drop in for an after-loss:
Ah! do not, when my heart hath 'scap'd this sorrow,
Come in the rearward of a conquer'd woe;
Give not a windy night a rainy morrow,
To linger out a purpos'd overthrow.
If thou wilt leave me, do not leave me last,
When other petty griefs have done their spite,
But in the onset come: so shall I taste
At first the very worst of fortune's might;
    And other strains of woe, which now seem woe,
    Compar'd with loss of thee will not seem so.

WILLIAM SHAKESPEARE

Three Things

'O cruel Death, give three things back,'
Sang a bone upon the shore;
'A child found all a child can lack,
Whether of pleasure or of rest,
Upon the abundance of my breast':
A bone wave-whitened and dried in the wind.

'Three dear things that women know,'
Sang a bone upon the shore;
'A man if I but held him so
When my body was alive
Found all the pleasure that life gave':
A bone wave-whitened and dried in the wind.

'The third thing that I think of yet,'
Sang a bone upon the shore,
'Is that morning when I met
Face to face my rightful man
And did after stretch and yawn':
A bone wave-whitened and dried in the wind.

W. B. YEATS

Within the Dream You Said

Within the dream you said:
Let us kiss then,
In this room, in this bed,
But when all's done
We must not meet again.

Hearing this last word,
There was no lambing-night,
No gale-driven bird
Nor frost-encircled root
As cold as my heart.

PHILIP LARKIN

94

Sonnet LXVI

Tir'd with all these, for restful death I cry,
As to behold desert a beggar born,
And needy nothing trimm'd in jollity,
And purest faith unhappily forsworn,
And gilded honour shamefully misplac'd,
And maiden virtue rudely strumpeted,
And right perfection wrongfully disgrac'd,
And strength by limping sway disabled,
And art made tongue-tied by authority,
And folly—doctor-like—controlling skill,
And simple truth miscall'd simplicity,
And captive good attending captain ill:
   Tir'd with all these, from these would I be gone,
   Save that, to die, I leave my love alone.

WILLIAM SHAKESPEARE

After Long Silence

Speech after long silence; it is right,
All other lovers being estranged or dead,
Unfriendly lamplight hid under its shade,
The curtains drawn upon unfriendly night,
That we descant and yet again descant
Upon the supreme theme of Art and Song:
Bodily decrepitude is wisdom; young
We loved each other and were ignorant.

W. B. YEATS

I Look into My Glass

I look into my glass,
And view my wasting skin,
And say, 'Would God it came to pass
My heart had shrunk as thin!'

For then, I, undistrest
By hearts grown cold to me,
Could lonely wait my endless rest
With equanimity.

But Time, to make me grieve,
Part steals, lets part abide;
And shakes this fragile frame at eve
With throbbings of noontide.

THOMAS HARDY

Jenny Kiss'd Me

Jenny kiss'd me when we met,
   Jumping from the chair she sat in;
Time, you thief, who love to get
   Sweets into your list, put that in!
Say I'm weary, say I'm sad,
   Say that health and wealth have miss'd me,
Say I'm growing old, but add,
   Jenny kiss'd me.

LEIGH HUNT

A Song of a Young Lady
To her Ancient Lover

I

Ancient Person, for whom I,
All the flatt'ring Youth defy;
Long be it e're thou grow Old,
Aking, shaking, Crazy Cold.
But still continue as thou art,
Ancient Person of My Heart.

2

On thy wither'd Lips and dry,
Which like barren Furrows lye,
Brooding Kisses I will pour,
Shall thy youthful Heart restore.
Such kind Show'rs in Autumn fall,
And a second Spring recall:
Nor from thee will ever part,
Ancient Person of my Heart.

3

Thy Nobler Part(s), which but to name,
In our Sex wou'd be counted shame,
By Ages frozen grasp possest,
From their Ice shall be releast:
And, sooth'd by my reviving Hand,
In former Warmth and Vigor stand.
All a Lover's Wish can reach,
For thy Joy my Love shall teach:
And for thy Pleasure shall improve,
All that Art can add to Love.
Yet still I love thee without Art,
Ancient Person of my Heart.

JOHN WILMOT,
EARL OF ROCHESTER

Politics

'In our time the destiny of man presents its meaning in political terms.'—THOMAS MANN

How can I, that girl standing there,
My attention fix
On Roman or on Russian
Or on Spanish politics?
Yet here's a travelled man that knows
What he talks about,
And there's a politician
That has read and thought,
And maybe what they say is true
Of war and war's alarms,
But O that I were young again
And held her in my arms!

W. B. YEATS

A Short Song of Congratulation

Long-expected one and twenty
Ling'ring year at last is flown,
Pomp and Pleasure, Pride and Plenty
Great Sir John, are all your own.

Loosen'd from the Minor's tether,
Free to mortgage or to sell,
Wild as wind, and light as feather
Bid the slaves of thrift farewel.

Call the Bettys, Kates, and Jennys
Ev'ry name that laughs at Care,
Lavish of your Grandsire's guineas,
Show the Spirit of an heir.

All that prey on vice and folly
Joy to see their quarry fly,
Here the Gamester light and jolly
There the Lender grave and sly.

98

Wealth, Sir John, was made to wander,
Let it wander as it will;
See the Jocky, see the Pander,
Bid them come, and take their fill.

When the bonny Blade carouses,
Pockets full, and Spirits high,
What are acres? what are houses?
Only dirt, or wet or dry.

If the Guardian or the Mother
Tell the woes of wilful waste,
Scorn their counsel and their pother,
You can hang or drown at last.

SAMUEL JOHNSON

Epistle

To Miss Blount, on her leaving the Town, after the Coronation

As some fond virgin, whom her mother's care
Drags from the town to wholsom country air,
Just when she learns to roll a melting eye,
And hear a spark, yet think no danger nigh;
From the dear man unwilling she must sever,
Yet takes one kiss before she parts for ever:
Thus from the world fair *Zephalinda* flew,
Saw others happy, and with sighs withdrew;
Not that their pleasures caus'd her discontent,
She sigh'd not that They stay'd, but that She went.
 She went, to plain-work, and to purling brooks,
Old-fashion'd halls, dull aunts, and croaking rooks,
She went from Op'ra, park, assembly, play,
To morning walks, and pray'rs three hours a day;

To pass her time 'twixt reading and Bohea,
To muse, and spill her solitary Tea,
Or o'er cold coffee trifle with the spoon,
Count the slow clock, and dine exact at noon;
Divert her eyes with pictures in the fire,
Hum half a tune, tell stories to the squire;
Up to her godly garret after sev'n,
There starve and pray, for that's the way to heav'n.

Some Squire, perhaps, you take delight to rack;
Whose game is Whisk, whose treat a toast in sack,
Who visits with a gun, presents you birds,
Then gives a smacking buss, and cries—No works!
Or with his hound comes hollowing from the stable,
Makes love with nods, and knees beneath a table;
Whose laughs are hearty, tho' his jests are coarse,
And loves you best of all things—but his horse.

In some fair evening, on your elbow laid,
You dream of triumphs in the rural shade;
In pensive thought recall the fancy'd scene,
See Coronations rise on ev'ry green;
Before you pass th' imaginary sights
Of Lords, and Earls, and Dukes, and garter'd Knights;
While the spread Fan o'ershades your closing eyes;
Then give one flirt, and all the vision flies.
Thus vanish sceptres, coronets, and balls,
And leave you in lone woods, or empty walls.

So when your slave, at some dear, idle time,
(Not plagu'd with headachs, or the want of rhime)
Stands in the streets, abstracted from the crew,
And while he seems to study, thinks of you:
Just when his fancy points your sprightly eyes,
Or sees the blush of soft *Parthenia* rise,
Gay pats my shoulder, and you vanish quite;
Streets, chairs, and coxcombs rush upon my sight;
Vext to be still in town, I knit my brow,
Look sow'r, and hum a tune—as you may now.

ALEXANDER POPE

Sonnet CXXVIII

How oft, when thou, my music, music play'st,
Upon that blessed wood whose motion sounds
With thy sweet fingers, when thou gently sway'st
The wiry concord that mine ear confounds,
Do I envy those jacks that nimble leap
To kiss the tender inward of thy hand,
Whilst my poor lips, which should that harvest reap,
At the wood's boldness by thee blushing stand!
To be so tickled, they would change their state
And situation with those dancing chips,
O'er whom thy fingers walk with gentle gait,
Making dead wood more bless'd than living lips.
   Since saucy jacks so happy are in this,
     Give them thy fingers, me thy lips to kiss.

WILLIAM SHAKESPEARE

From The Miller's Tale

   Fair was this yonge wyf, and therwithal
As any wezele hir body gent and smal.
A ceynt she werede, barred al of silk,
A barmclooth eek as whit as morne milk
Upon hir lendes, ful of many a goore.
Whit was hir smok, and broyden al bifoore
And eek bihynde, on hir coler aboute,
Of col-blak silk, withinne and eek withoute.
The tapes of hir white voluper
Were of the same suyte of hir coler;
Hir filet brood of silk, and set ful hye.
And sikerly she hadde a likerous ye;
Ful smale ypulled were hire browes two,
And tho were bent and blake as any sloo.
She was full moore blisful on to see

Than is the newe-pere-jonette tree,
And softer than the wolle is of a wether.
And by hir girdel heeng a purs of lether,
Tasseled with silk, and perled with latoun.
In al this world, to seken up and doun,
There nys no man so wys that koude thenche
So gay a popelote or swich a wenche.
Ful brighter was the shynyng of hir hewe
Than in the tour the noble yforged newe.
But of hir song, it was as loude and yerne
As any swalwe sittynge on a berne.
Therto she koude skippe and make game,
As any kyde or calf folwynge his dame.
Hir mouth was sweete as bragot or the meeth,
Or hoord of apples leyd in hey or heeth.
Wynsynge she was, as is a joly colt,
Long as a mast, and upright as a bolt.
A brooch she baar upon hir lowe coler,
As brood as is the boos of a bokeler.
Hir shoes were laced on hir legges hye.
She was a prymerole, a piggesnye,
For any lord to leggen in his bedde,
Or yet for any good yeman to wedde.

GEOFFREY CHAUCER

The River-Merchant's Wife: A Letter

While my hair was still cut straight across my forehead
I played about the front gate, pulling flowers.
You came by on bamboo stilts, playing horse,
You walked about my seat, playing with blue plums.
And we went on living in the village of Chokan:
Two small people, without dislike or suspicion.

At fourteen I married My Lord you.
I never laughed, being bashful.
Lowering my head, I looked at the wall.
Called to, a thousand times, I never looked back.

At fifteen I stopped scowling,
I desired my dust to be mingled with yours
Forever and forever and forever.
Why should I climb the look out?

At sixteen you departed,
You went into far Ku-to-yen, by the river of swirling eddies,
And you have been gone five months.
The monkeys make sorrowful noise overhead.

You dragged your feet when you went out.
By the gate now, the moss is grown, the different mosses,
Too deep to clear them away!
The leaves fall early this autumn, in wind.
The paired butterflies are already yellow with August
Over the grass in the West garden;
They hurt me. I grow older.
If you are coming down through the narrows of the river
        Kiang,
Please let me know beforehand,
And I will come out to meet you
                As far as Cho-fu-Sa.

                        By Rihaku

                    EZRA POUND

A Church Romance

(Mellstock: circa 1835)

She turned in the high pew, until her sight
Swept the west gallery, and caught its row
Of music-men with viol, book, and bow
Against the sinking sad tower-window light.

She turned again; and in her pride's despite
One strenuous viol's inspirer seemed to throw
A message from his string to her below,
Which said: 'I claim thee as my own forthright!'

Thus their hearts' bond began, in due time signed.
And long years thence, when Age had scared Romance,
At some old attitude of his or glance
That gallery-scene would break upon her mind,
With him as minstrel, ardent, young, and trim,
Bowing 'New Sabbath' or 'Mount Ephraim'.

THOMAS HARDY

Henry IV, Part I (Act III, sc i)

MORTIMER: This is the deadly spite that angers me:
              My wife can speak no English, I no Welsh.
GLENDOWER: My daughter weeps: she'll not part with
              you;
She'll be a soldier too, she'll to the wars.
MORTIMER: Good father, tell her that she and my aunt
              Percy
Shall follow in your conduct speedily.
  [*Glendower speaks to her in Welsh, and she answers
  him in the same.*

GLENDOWER: She is desperate here; a peevish self-will'd
harlotry, one that no persuasion can do good upon.
[*The Lady speaks in Welsh.*
MORTIMER: I understand thy looks: that pretty Welsh
Which thou pourest down from these swelling heavens
I am too perfect in; and, but for shame,
In such a parley should I answer thee.
[*The Lady speaks again in Welsh.*
I understand thy kisses, and thou mine,
And that's a feeling disputation;
But I will never be a truant, love,
Till I have learnt thy language; for thy tongue
Makes Welsh as sweet as ditties highly penn'd,
Sung by a fair queen in a summer's bow'r,
With ravishing division, to her lute.
GLENDOWER: Nay, if you melt, then will she run mad.
[*The Lady speaks again in Welsh.*
MORTIMER: O, I am ignorance itself in this!
GLENDOWER: She bids you on the wanton rushes lay you
down,
And rest your gentle head upon her lap,
And she will sing the song that pleaseth you,
And on your eyelids crown the god of sleep,
Charming your blood with pleasing heaviness,
Making such difference 'twixt wake and sleep
As is the difference betwixt day and night
The hour before the heavenly-harness'd team
Begins his golden progress in the east.
MORTIMER: With all my heart I'll sit and hear her sing;
By that time will our book, I think, be drawn.
GLENDOWER: Do so;
And those musicians that shall play to you
Hang in the air a thousand leagues from hence,
And straight they shall be here; sit, and attend.

WILLIAM SHAKESPEARE

From Paradise Lost (Book IX)

                              Adam the while
Waiting desirous her return, had wove
Of choicest Flours a Garland to adorne
Her Tresses, and her rural labours crown
As Reapers oft are wont thir Harvest Queen.
Great joy he promis'd to his thoughts, and new
Solace in her return, so long delay'd;
Yet oft his heart, divine of somthing ill,
Misgave him; hee the faultring measure felt;
And forth to meet her went, the way she took
That Morn when first they parted; by the Tree
Of Knowledge he must pass, there he her met,
Scarse from the Tree returning; in her hand
A bough of fairest fruit that downie smil'd,
New gatherd, and ambrosial smell diffus'd.
To him she hasted, in her face excuse
Came Prologue, and Apologie to prompt,
Which with bland words at will she thus addrest.
    Hast thou not wondered, *Adam*, at my stay?
Thee I have misst, and thought it long, depriv'd
Thy presence, agonie of love till now
Not felt, nor shall be twice, for never more
Mean I to trie, what rash untri'd I sought,
The paine of absence from thy sight. But strange
Hath bin the cause, and wonderful to heare:
This Tree is not as we are told, a Tree
Of danger tasted, nor to evil unknown
Op'ning the way, but of Divine effect
To open Eyes, and make them Gods who taste;
And hath bin tasted such: the Serpent wise,
Or not restraind as wee, or not obeying,
Hath eat'n of the fruit, and is become,
Not dead, as we are threatn'd, but thenceforth
Endu'd with human voice and human sense,
Reasoning to admiration, and with mee
Perswasively hath so prevaild, that I

Have also tasted, and have also found
Th' effects to correspond, opener mine Eyes,
Dimm erst, dilated Spirits, ampler Heart,
And growing up to Godhead; which for thee
Chiefly I sought, without thee can despise.
For bliss, as thou hast part, to me is bliss,
Tedious, unshar'd with thee, and odious soon.
Thou therfore also taste, that equal Lot
May joyne us, equal Joy, as equal Love;
Least thou not tasting, different degree
Disjoyne us, and I then too late renounce
Deitie for thee, when Fate will not permit.

    Thus *Eve* with Countnance blithe her storie told;
But in her Cheek distemper flushing glowd.
On th' other side, *Adam*, soon as he heard
The fatal Trespass don by *Eve*, amaz'd,
Astonied stood and Blank, while horror chill
Ran through his veins, and all his joynts relax'd;
From his slack hand the Garland wreath'd for *Eve*
Down drop'd, and all the faded Roses shed:
Speechless he stood and pale, till thus at length
First to himself he inward silence broke.

    O fairest of Creation, last and best
Of all Gods Works, Creature in whom excell'd
Whatever can to sight or thought be formd,
Holy, divine, good, amiable, or sweet!
How art thou lost, how on a sudden lost,
Defac't, deflourd, and now to Death devote?
Rather how hast thou yeelded to transgress
The strict forbiddance, how to violate
The sacred Fruit forbidd'n! som cursed fraud
Of Enemie hath beguil'd thee, yet unknown,
And mee with thee hath ruind, for with thee
Certain my resolution is to Die;
How can I live without thee, how forgoe
Thy sweet Converse and Love so dearly joyn'd,
To live again in these wilde Woods forlorn?
Should God create another *Eve*, and I

Another Rib afford, yet loss of thee
Would never from my heart; no no, I feel
The Link of Nature draw me: Flesh of Flesh,
Bone of my Bone thou art, and from thy State
Mine never shall be parted, bliss or woe.

JOHN MILTON

An Epitaph Upon a Married Couple

Dead and buried together

To these, whom Death again did wed,
This grave's their second marriage-bed;
For though the hand of Fate could force
'Twixt soul and body a divorce,
It could not sunder man and wife,
Because they both lived but one life.
Peace, good Reader, do not weep.
Peace, the lovers are asleep.
They, sweet turtles, folded lie
In the last knot Love could tie.
And though they lie as they were dead,
Their pillow stone, their sheets of lead,
(Pillow hard, and sheets not warm)
Love made the bed; they'll take no harm.
Let them sleep: let them sleep on,
Till this stormy night be gone,
Till the eternal morrow dawn;
Then the curtains will be drawn
And they wake into a light,
Whose day shall never die in night.

RICHARD CRASHAW

The Going

Why did you give no hint that night
That quickly after the morrow's dawn,
And calmly, as if indifferent quite,
You would close your term here, up and be gone
    Where I could not follow
    With wing of swallow
To gain one glimpse of you ever anon!

    Never to bid good-bye,
    Or lip me the softest call,
Or utter a wish for a word, while I
Saw morning harden upon the wall,
    Unmoved, unknowing
    That your great going
Had place that moment, and altered all.

Why do you make me leave the house
And think for a breath it is you I see
At the end of the alley of bending boughs
Where so often at dusk you used to be;
    Till in darkening dankness
    The yawning blankness
Of the perspective sickens me!

    You were she who abode
    By those red-veined rocks far West,
You were the swan-necked one who rode
Along the beetling Beeny Crest,
    And, reining nigh me,
    Would muse and eye me,
While Life unrolled us its very best.

Why, then, latterly did we not speak,
Did we not think of those days long dead,
And ere your vanishing strive to seek
That time's renewal? We might have said,
    'In this bright spring weather
    We'll visit together
Those places that once we visited.'

    Well, well! All's past amend,
    Unchangeable. It must go.
I seem but a dead man held on end
To sink down soon. . . . O you could not know
    That such swift fleeing
    No soul foreseeing –
Not even I – would undo me so!

THOMAS HARDY

Sonnet XIX

Methought I saw my late espoused Saint
    Brought to me like *Alcestis* from the grave,
    Whom *Joves* great Son to her glad Husband gave,
    Rescu'd from death by force though pale and faint.
Mine as whom washt from spot of child-bed taint,
    Purification in the old Law did save,
    And such, as yet once more I trust to have
    Full sight of her in Heaven without restraint,
Came vested all in white, pure as her mind:
    Her face was vail'd, yet to my fancied sight,
    Love, sweetness, goodness, in her person shin'd
So clear, as in no face with more delight.
    But O as to embrace me she enclin'd
    I wak'd, she fled, and day brought back my night.

JOHN MILTON

At Castle Boterel

As I drive to the junction of lane and highway,
    And the drizzle bedrenches the waggonette,
I look behind at the fading byway,
    And see on its slope, now glistening wet,
        Distinctly yet

Myself and a girlish form benighted
    In dry March weather. We climb the road
Beside a chaise. We had just alighted
    To ease the sturdy pony's load
        When he sighed and slowed.

What we did as we climbed, and what we talked of
    Matters not much, nor to what it led, –
Something that life will not be balked of
    Without rude reason till hope is dead,
        And feeling fled.

It filled but a minute. But was there ever
    A time of such quality, since or before,
In that hill's story? To one mind never,
    Though it has been climbed, foot-swift, foot-sore,
        By thousands more.

Primaeval rocks form the road's steep border,
    And much have they faced there, first and last,
Of the transitory in Earth's long order;
    But what they record in colour and cast
        Is – that we two passed.

And to me, though Time's unflinching rigour,
    In mindless rote, has ruled from sight
The substance now, one phantom figure
    Remains on the slope, as when that night
        Saw us alight.

I look and see it there, shrinking, shrinking,
   I look back at it amid the rain
For the very last time; for my sand is sinking,
   And I shall traverse old love's domain
      Never again.

THOMAS HARDY

Othello (Act I, sc iii)

OTHELLO: Her father lov'd me, oft invited me;
Still question'd me the story of my life
From year to year—the battles, sieges, fortunes,
That I have pass'd.
I ran it through, even from my boyish days
To th' very moment that he bade me tell it;
Wherein I spake of most disastrous chances,
Of moving accidents by flood and field;
Of hairbreadth scapes i' th' imminent deadly breach;
Of being taken by the insolent foe
And sold to slavery; of my redemption thence,
And portance in my travel's history;
Wherein of antres vast and deserts idle,
Rough quarries, rocks, and hills whose heads touch
     heaven,
It was my hint to speak—such was the process;
And of the Cannibals that each other eat,
The Anthropophagi, and men whose heads
Do grow beneath their shoulders. This to hear
Would Desdemona seriously incline;
But still the house affairs would draw her thence;
Which ever as she could with haste dispatch,
She'd come again, and with a greedy ear
Devour up my discourse. Which I observing,
Took once a pliant hour, and found good means
To draw from her a prayer of earnest heart
That I would all my pilgrimage dilate,

Whereof by parcels she had something heard,
But not intentively. I did consent,
And often did beguile her of her tears,
When I did speak of some distressful stroke
That my youth suffer'd. My story being done,
She gave me for my pains a world of sighs;
She swore, in faith, 'twas strange, 'twas passing strange;
'Twas pitiful, 'twas wondrous pitiful.
She wish'd she had not heard it; yet she wish'd
That heaven had made her such a man. She thank'd me;
And bade me, if I had a friend that lov'd her,
I should but teach him how to tell my story,
And that would woo her. Upon this hint I spake;
She lov'd me for the dangers I had pass'd;
And I lov'd her that she did pity them.
This only is the witchcraft I have us'd.

WILLIAM SHAKESPEARE

An Acre of Grass

Picture and book remain,
An acre of green grass
For air and exercise,
Now strength of body goes;
Midnight, an old house
Where nothing stirs but a mouse.

My temptation is quiet.
Here at life's end
Neither loose imagination,
Nor the mill of the mind
Consuming its rag and bone,
Can make the truth known.

Grant me an old man's frenzy,
Myself must I remake
Till I am Timon and Lear
Or that William Blake
Who beat upon the wall
Till Truth obeyed his call;

A mind Michael Angelo knew
That can pierce the clouds,
Or inspired by frenzy
Shake the dead in their shrouds;
Forgotten else by mankind,
An old man's eagle mind.

W. B. YEATS

Timon of Athens (Act IV, sc iii)

TIMON: Put up thy gold. Go on. Here's gold. Go on.
Be as a planetary plague, when Jove
Will o'er some high-vic'd city hang his poison
In the sick air; let not thy sword skip one.
Pity not honour'd age for his white beard:
He is an usurer. Strike me the counterfeit matron:
It is her habit only that is honest,
Herself's a bawd. Let not the virgin's cheek
Make soft thy trenchant sword; for those milk paps
That through the window bars bore at men's eyes
Are not within the leaf of pity writ,
But set them down horrible traitors. Spare not the babe
Whose dimpled smiles from fools exhaust their mercy;
Think it a bastard whom the oracle
Hath doubtfully pronounc'd thy throat shall cut,
And mince it sans remorse. Swear against abjects;
Put armour on thine ears and on thine eyes,
Whose proof nor yells of mothers, maids, nor babes,

Nor sight of priests in holy vestments bleeding,
Shall pierce a jot. There's gold to pay thy soldiers.
Make large confusion; and, thy fury spent,
Confounded be thyself! Speak not, be gone.

ALCIBIADES: Hast thou gold yet? I'll take the gold thou
givest me,
Not all thy counsel.

TIMON: Dost thou, or dost thou not, heaven's
curse upon thee!

PHRYNIA AND Give us some gold, good Timon. Hast thou
TIMANDRA: more?

TIMON: Enough to make a whore forswear her
trade,
And to make whores a bawd. Hold up, you sluts,
Your aprons mountant; you are not oathable,
Although I know you'll swear, terribly swear,
Into strong shudders and to heavenly agues,
Th' immortal gods that hear you. Spare your oaths;
I'll trust to your conditions. Be whores still;
And he whose pious breath seeks to convert you—
Be strong in whore, allure him, burn him up;
Let your close fire predominate his smoke,
And be no turncoats. Yet may your pains six months
Be quite contrary! And thatch your poor thin roofs
With burdens of the dead—some that were hang'd,
No matter. Wear them, betray with them. Whore still;
Paint till a horse may mire upon your face.
A pox of wrinkles!

WILLIAM SHAKESPEARE

The Winter's Tale (Act I, sc ii)

HERMIONE: If you would seek us,
We are yours i' th' garden. Shall's attend you there?
LEONTES: To your own bents dispose you; you'll be found,
Be you beneath the sky. [*Aside*] I am angling now,
Though you perceive me not how I give line.
Go to, go to!
How she holds up the neb, the bill to him!
And arms her with the boldness of a wife
To her allowing husband! [*Exeunt Polixenes, Hermione,
    and Attendants.*] Gone already!
Inch-thick, knee-deep, o'er head and ears a fork'd one!
Go, play, boy, play; thy mother plays, and I
Play too; but so disgrac'd a part, whose issue
Will hiss me to my grave. Contempt and clamour
Will be my knell. Go, play, boy, play. There have been,
Or I am much deceiv'd, cuckolds ere now;
And many a man there is, even at this present,
Now while I speak this, holds his wife by th' arm
That little thinks she has been sluic'd in's absence,
And his pond fish'd by his next neighbour, by
Sir Smile, his neighbour. Nay, there's comfort in't,
Whiles other men have gates and those gates open'd,
As mine, against their will. Should all despair
That have revolted wives, the tenth of mankind
Would hang themselves. Physic for't there's none;
It is a bawdy planet, that will strike
Where 'tis predominant; and 'tis pow'rful, think it,
From east, west, north, and south. Be it concluded,
No barricado for a belly. Know't,
It will let in and out the enemy
With bag and baggage. Many thousand on's
Have the disease, and feel't not. How now boy!
MAMILLIUS: I am like you, they say.
LEONTES: Why, that's some comfort.

WILLIAM SHAKESPEARE

Othello (Act III, sc iii)

OTHELLO: I had been happy if the general camp,
Pioneers and all, had tasted her sweet body,
So I had nothing known. O, now for ever
Farewell the tranquil mind! farewell content!
Farewell the plumed troops, and the big wars
That makes ambition virtue! O, farewell!
Farewell the neighing steed and the shrill trump,
The spirit-stirring drum, th' ear-piercing fife,
The royal banner, and all quality,
Pride, pomp, and circumstance, of glorious war!
And O ye mortal engines whose rude throats
Th' immortal Jove's dread clamours counterfeit,
Farewell! Othello's occupation's gone.

WILLIAM SHAKESPEARE

Macbeth (Act V, sc v)

MACBETH: . . . What is that noise?
SEYTON: It is the cry of women, my good lord.
                                                                    [*Exit*
MACBETH: I have almost forgot the taste of fears.
The time has been my senses would have cool'd
To hear a night-shriek, and my fell of hair
Would at a dismal treatise rouse and stir
As life were in't. I have supp'd full with horrors;
Direness, familiar to my slaughterous thoughts,
Cannot once start me.
Re-enter SEYTON.
                                  Wherefore was that cry?
SEYTON: The Queen, my lord, is dead.
MACBETH: She should have died hereafter;
There would have been a time for such a word.
To-morrow, and to-morrow, and to-morrow,

Creeps in this petty pace from day to day
To the last syllable of recorded time,
And all our yesterdays have lighted fools
The way to dusty death. Out, out, brief candle!
Life's but a walking shadow, a poor player,
That struts and frets his hour upon the stage,
And then is heard no more; it is a tale
Told by an idiot, full of sound and fury,
Signifying nothing.

WILLIAM SHAKESPEARE

Mutability

From low to high doth dissolution climb,
And sink from high to low, along a scale
Of awful notes, whose concord shall not fail;
A musical but melancholy chime,
Which they can hear who meddle not with crime,
Nor avarice, nor over-anxious care.
Truth fails not; but her outward forms that bear
The longest date do melt like frosty rime,
That in the morning whitened hill and plain
And is no more; drop like the tower sublime
Of yesterday, which royally did wear
His crown of weeds, but could not even sustain
Some casual shout that broke the silent air,
Or the unimaginable touch of Time.

WILLIAM WORDSWORTH

Ah! Sunflower

Ah, Sunflower! weary of time,
Who countest the steps of the Sun;
Seeking after that sweet golden clime,
Where the traveller's journey is done;

Where the Youth pined away with desire,
And the pale Virgin shrouded in snow,
Arise from their graves, and aspire
Where my Sunflower wishes to go.

WILLIAM BLAKE

Leaves of Grass

(40)

Flaunt of the sunshine I need not your bask—lie over!
You light surfaces only, I force surfaces and depths also.

Earth! you seem to look for something at my hands,
Say, old top-knot, what do you want?

Man or woman, I might tell how I like you, but cannot,
And might tell what it is in me and what it is in you, but
    cannot,
And might tell that pining I have, that pulse of my nights
    and days.

Behold, I do not give lectures or a little charity,
When I give I give myself.

You there, impotent, loose in the knees,
Open your scarf'd chops till I blow grit within you,
Spread your palms and lift the flaps of your pockets,
I am not to be denied, I compel, I have stores plenty and to
    spare,
And any thing I have I bestow.

I do not ask who you are, that is not important to me,
You can do nothing and be nothing but what I will infold
    you.

To cotton-field drudge or cleaner of privies I lean,
On his right cheek I put the family kiss,
And in my soul I swear I never will deny him.

On women fit for conception I start bigger and nimbler
    babes.
(This day I am jetting the stuff of far more arrogant
    republics.)

To any one dying, thither I speed and twist the knob of the
    door,
Turn the bed-clothes toward the foot of the bed,
Let the physician and the priest go home.

I seize the descending man and raise him with resistless will,
O despairer, here is my neck,
By God, you shall not go down! hang your whole weight
    upon me.

I dilate you with tremendous breath, I buoy you up,
Every room of the house do I fill with an arm'd force,
Lovers of me, bafflers of graves.

Sleep—I and they keep guard all night,
Not doubt, not decease shall dare to lay finger upon you,
I have embraced you, and henceforth possess you to myself,
And when you rise in the morning you will find what I
    tell you is so.

WALT WHITMAN

From Paradise Lost (Book III)

Hail holy light, ofspring of Heav'n first-born,
Or of th' Eternal Coeternal beam
May I express thee unblam'd? since God is light,
And never but in unapproached light
Dwelt from Eternitie, dwelt then in thee,
Bright effluence of bright essence increate.
Or hear'st thou rather pure Ethereal stream,
Whose Fountain who shall tell? before the Sun,
Before the Heavens thou wert, and at the voice
Of God, as with a Mantle didst invest
The rising world of waters dark and deep,
Won from the void and formless infinite.
Thee I re-visit now with bolder wing,
Escap't the *Stygian* Pool, though long detain'd
In that obscure sojourn, while in my flight
Through utter and through middle darkness borne
With other notes then to th' *Orphean* Lyre
I sung of *Chaos* and *Eternal Night*,
Taught by the heav'nly Muse to venture down
The dark descent, and up to reascend,
Though hard and rare: thee I revisit safe,
And feel thy sovran vital Lamp; but thou
Revisit'st not these eyes, that rowle in vain
To find thy piercing ray, and find no dawn;
So thick a drop serene hath quencht thir Orbs,
Or dim suffusion veild. Yet not the more
Cease I to wander where the Muses haunt
Cleer Spring, or shadie Grove, or Sunnie Hill,
Smit with the love of sacred song; but chief
Thee *Sion* and the flowrie Brooks beneath
That wash thy hallowd feet, and warbling flow,
Nightly I visit: nor somtimes forget
Those other two equal'd with me in Fate,
So were I equal'd with them in renown,
Blind *Thamyris* and blind *Mæonides*,
And *Tiresias* and *Phineus* Prophets old.

Then feed on thoughts, that voluntarie move
Harmonious numbers; as the wakeful Bird
Sings darkling, and in shadiest Covert hid
Tunes her nocturnal Note. Thus with the Year
Seasons return, but not to me returns
Day, or the sweet approach of Ev'n or Morn,
Or sight of vernal bloom, or Summers Rose,
Or flocks, or herds, or human face divine;
But cloud in stead, and ever-during dark
Surrounds me, from the chearful waies of men
Cut off, and for the Book of knowledg fair
Presented with a Universal blanc
Of Natures works to mee expung'd and ras'd,
And wisdome at one entrance quite shut out.
So much the rather thou Celestial light
Shine inward, and the mind through all her powers
Irradiate, there plant eyes, all mist from thence
Purge and disperse, that I may see and tell
Of things invisible to mortal sight.

JOHN MILTON

Thou Art Indeed Just

*Justus quidem tu es, Domine, si disputem tecum:
verumtamen justa loquar ad te: Quare via impiorum
prosperatur? &c.*

Thou art indeed just, Lord, if I contend
With thee; but, sir, so what I plead is just.
Why do sinners' ways prosper? and why must
Disappointment all I endeavour end?
    Wert thou my enemy, O thou my friend,
How wouldst thou worse, I wonder, than thou dost
Defeat, thwart me? Oh, the sots and thralls of lust
Do in spare hours more thrive than I that spend,

Sir, life upon thy cause. See, banks and brakes
Now, leavèd how thick! lacèd they are again
With fretty chervil, look, and fresh wind shakes
Them; birds build—but not I build; no, but strain,
Time's eunuch, and not breed one work that wakes.
Mine, O thou lord of life, send my roots rain.

GERARD MANLEY HOPKINS

Redemption

Having been tenant long to a rich Lord,
    Not thriving, I resolved to be bold,
    And make a suit unto him, to afford
A new small-rented lease, and cancell th' old.
In heaven at his manour I him sought:
    They told me there, that he was lately gone
    About some land, which he had dearly bought
Long since on earth, to take possession.
I straight return'd, and knowing his great birth,
    Sought him accordingly in great resorts;
    In cities, theatres, gardens, parks, and courts:
At length I heard a ragged noise and mirth
    Of theeves and murderers: there I him espied,
    Who straight, *Your suit is granted*, said, & died.

GEORGE HERBERT

Was He Married?

Was he married, did he try
To support as he grew less fond of them
Wife and family?

No,
He never suffered such a blow.

Did he feel pointless, feeble and distrait,
Unwanted by everyone and in the way?

From his cradle he was purposeful,
His bent strong and his mind full.

Did he love people very much
Yet find them die one day?

He did not love in the human way.

Did he ask how long it would go on,
Wonder if Death could be counted on for an end?

He did not feel like this,
He had a future of bliss.

Did he never feel strong
Pain for being wrong?

He was not wrong, he was right,
He suffered from others', not his own, spite.

But there *is* no suffering like having made a mistake
Because of being of an inferior make.

He was not inferior,
He was superior.

He knew then that power corrupts but some must govern?

His thoughts were different.

Did he lack friends? Worse,
Think it was for his fault, not theirs?

He did not lack friends,
He had disciples he moulded to his ends.

Did he feel over-handicapped sometimes, yet must draw
        even?

How could he feel like this? He was the King of Heaven

. . . find a sudden brightness one day in everything
Because a mood had been conquered, or a sin?

I tell you, he did not sin.

Do only human beings suffer from the irritation
I have mentioned? learn too that being comical
Does not ameliorate the desperation?

Only human beings feel this,
It is because they are so mixed.

All human beings should have a medal,
A god cannot carry it, he is not able.

A god is Man's doll, you ass,
He makes him up like this on purpose.

He might have made him up worse.

He often has, in the past.

To choose a god of love, as he did and does,
Is a little move then?

Yes, it is.

A larger one will be when men
Love love and hate hate but do not deify them?

It will be a larger one.

STEVIE SMITH

He Bare Him Up

Lully, lulley, lully, lulley,
The faucon hath borne my make away.

He bare him up, he bare him down,
He bare him into an orchard brown.

In that orchard there was an halle,
That was hanged with purpill and pall.

And in that hall there was a bede,
It was hanged with gold so rede.

And in that bed there lithe a knight,
His woundes bleding day and night.

By that bede side kneleth a may,
And she wepeth both night and day.

And by that bede side there stondeth a stone,
Corpus Christi wreten there on.

ANON

Thanks and a Plea to Mary

Levedy, ic thonke thee,
Wid herte swithe milde,
That god that thu havest idon me
Wid thine swete childe.

Thu art god and swete and bright,
Of alle otheir icoren.
Of thee was that swete wight,
That was Jesus, iboren.

Maide milde, bidd I thee
Wid thine swete childe,
That thu herdie me
To habben Godis milce.

Moder, loke one me,
Wid thine swete eyen,
Reste and blisse gef thu me,
My levedy, then ic deyen.

ANON

Leaves of Grass

(38)

Enough! enough! enough!
Somehow I have been stunn'd. Stand back!
Give me a little time beyond my cuff'd head, slumbers,
    dreams, gaping,
I discover myself on the verge of a usual mistake.

That I could forget the mockers and insults!
That I could forget the trickling tears and the blows of the
    bludgeons and hammers!
That I could look with a separate look on my own
    crucifixion and bloody crowning.

I remember now,
I resume the overstaid fraction,
The grave of rock multiplies what has been confided to it,
    or to any graves,
Corpses rise, gashes heal, fastenings roll from me.

I troop forth replenish'd with supreme power, one of an
    average unending procession,
Inland and sea-coast we go, and pass all boundary lines,
Our swift ordinances on their way over the whole earth,
The blossoms we wear in our hats the growth of thousands
    of years.

Eleves, I salute you! come forward!
Continue your annotations, continue your questionings.

WALT WHITMAN

Love (III)

Love bade me welcome: yet my soul drew back,
    Guiltie of dust and sinne.
But quick-ey'd Love, observing me grow slack
    From my first entrance in,
Drew nearer to me, sweetly questioning,
    If I lack'd any thing.

A guest, I answer'd, worthy to be here:
    Love said, You shall be he.
I the unkinde, ungratefull? Ah my deare,
    I cannot look on thee.
Love took my hand, and smiling did reply,
    Who made the eyes but I?

Truth Lord, but I have marr'd them: let my shame
    Go where it doth deserve.
And know you not, sayes Love, who bore the blame?
    My deare, then I will serve.
You must sit down, sayes Love, and taste my meat:
    So I did seat and eat.

GEORGE HERBERT

Jordan (I)

Who sayes that fictions onely and false hair
Become a verse? Is there in truth no beautie?
Is all good structure in a winding stair?
May no lines passe, except they do their dutie
    Not to a true, but painted chair?

Is it no verse, except enchanted groves
And sudden arbours shadow course-spunne lines?
Must purling streams refresh a lovers loves?
Must all be vail'd, while he that reades, divines,
  Catching the sense at two removes?

Shepherds are honest people; let them sing:
Riddle who list, for me, and pull for Prime:
I envie no mans nightingale or spring;
Nor let them punish me with losse of rime,
  Who plainly say, *My God, My King.*

GEORGE HERBERT

The Habit of Perfection

Elected Silence, sing to me
And beat upon my whorlèd ear,
Pipe me to pastures still and be
The music that I care to hear.

Shape nothing, lips; be lovely-dumb:
It is the shut, the curfew sent
From there where all surrenders come
Which only makes you eloquent.

Be shellèd, eyes, with double dark
And find the uncreated light:
This ruck and reel which you remark
Coils, keeps, and teases simple sight.

Palate, the hutch of tasty lust,
Desire not to be rinsed with wine:
The can must be so sweet, the crust
So fresh that come in fasts divine!

Nostrils, your careless breath that spend
Upon the stir and keep of pride,
What relish shall the censers send
Along the sanctuary side!

O feel-of-primrose hands, O feet
That want the yield of plushy sward,
But you shall walk the golden street
And you unhouse and house the Lord.

And, Poverty, be thou the bride
And now the marriage feast begun,
And lily-coloured clothes provide
Your spouse not laboured-at nor spun.

GERARD MANLEY HOPKINS

Emblem IV

I am my beloved's, and his desire is towards me.

Like to the arctic needle, that doth guide
    The wandering shade by his magnetic power,
And leaves his silken gnomon to decide
    The question of the controverted hour,
First frantics up and down from side to side,
        And restless beats his crystalled ivory case
        With vain impatience; jets from place to place,
And seeks the bosom of his frozen bride;
        At length he slacks his motion, and doth rest
His trembling point at his bright pole's belovèd breast.

Even so my soul, being hurried here and there,
    By every object that presents delight,
Fain would be settled, but she knows not where;
    She likes at morning what she loathes at night:
She bows to honour, then she lends an ear
        To that sweet swan-like voice of dying pleasure,
        Then tumbles in the scattered heaps of treasure;
Now flattered with false hope, now foiled with fear:
        Thus finding all the world's delight to be
But empty toys, good God, she points alone to thee.

But hath the virtued steel a power to move?
    Or can the untouched needle point aright?
Or can my wandering thoughts forbear to rove,
    Unguided by the virtue of thy sprite?
Oh hath my laden soul the art to improve
        Her wasted talent, and, unraised, aspire
        In this sad moulting time of her desire?
Not first beloved, have I the power to love?
        I cannot stir but as thou please to move me,
Nor can my heart return thee love until thou love me.

The still commandress of the silent night
    Borrows her beams from her bright brother's eye;
His fair aspéct fills her sharp horns with light,
    If he withdraw, her flames are quenched and die:
Even so the beams of thy enlightening sprite,
        Infused and shot into my dark desire,
        Inflame my thoughts, and fill my soul with fire,
That I am ravished with a new delight;
    But if thou shroud thy face, my glory fades,
And I remain a nothing, all composed of shades.

Eternal God! O thou that only art,
   The sacred fountain of eternal light,
And blessed loadstone of my better part,
   O thou, my heart's desire, my soul's delight!
Reflect upon my soul, and touch my heart,
      And then my heart shall prize no good above thee;
      And then my soul shall know thee; knowing, love thee;
And then my trembling thoughts shall never start
      From thy commands, or swerve the least degree,
Or once presume to move, but as they move in thee.

FRANCIS QUARLES

Heaven-Haven

A nun takes the veil

   I have desired to go
      Where springs not fail,
To fields where flies no sharp and sided hail
   And a few lilies blow.

   And I have asked to be
      Where no storms come,
Where the green swell is in the havens dumb,
   And out of the swing of the sea.

GERARD MANLEY HOPKINS

The Pearl. Matt. 13, 45

I know the wayes of Learning; both the head
And pipes that feed the presse, and make it runne;
What reason hath from nature borrowed,
Or of it self, like a good huswife, spunne
In laws and policie; what the starres conspire,
What willing nature speaks, what forc'd by fire;
Both th' old discoveries, and the new-found seas,
The stock and surplus, cause and historie:
All these stand open, or I have the keyes:
       Yet I love thee.

I know the wayes of Honour, what maintains
The quick returns of courtesie and wit:
In vies of favours whether partie gains,
When glorie swells the heart, and moldeth it
To all expressions both of hand and eye,
Which on the world a true-love-knot may tie,
And bear the bundle, wheresoe're it goes:
How many drammes of spirit there must be
To sell my life unto my friends or foes:
       Yet I love thee.

I know the wayes of Pleasure, the sweet strains,
The lullings and the relishes of it;
The propositions of hot bloud and brains;
What mirth and musick mean; what love and wit
Have done these twentie hundred yeares, and more:
I know the projects of unbridled store:
My stuffe is flesh, not brasse; my senses live,
And grumble oft, that they have more in me
Then he that curbs them, being but one to five:
       Yet I love thee.

I know all these, and have them in my hand:
Therefore not sealed, but with open eyes
I flie to thee, and fully understand
Both the main sale, and the commodities;
And at what rate and price I have thy love;
With all the circumstances that may move:
Yet through these labyrinths, not my groveling wit,
But thy silk twist let down from heav'n to me,
Did both conduct and teach me, how by it
          To climbe to thee.

GEORGE HERBERT

A Hymn to Christ, at the Author's last going into Germany

In what torn ship soever I embark,
That ship shall be my emblem of thy ark;
What sea soever swallow me, that flood
Shall be to me an emblem of thy blood;
Though thou with clouds of anger do disguise
Thy face; yet through that mask I know those eyes,
   Which, though they turn away sometimes,
     They never will despise.

I sacrifice this Island unto thee,
And all whom I loved there, and who loved me;
When I have put our seas 'twixt them and me,
Put thou thy sea betwixt my sins and thee.
As the tree's sap doth seek the root below
In winter, in my winter now I go,
   Where none but thee, th' eternal root
     Of true love I may know.

Nor thou nor thy religion dost control,
The amorousness of an harmonious soul,
But thou wouldst have that love thyself: as thou
Art jealous, Lord, so I am jealous now,
Thou lov'st not, till from loving more, thou free
My soul; who ever gives, takes liberty:
 O, if thou car'st not whom I love
  Alas, thou lov'st not me.

Seal then this bill of my divorce to all,
On whom those fainter beams of love did fall;
Marry those loves, which in youth scattered be
On fame, wit, hopes (false mistresses) to thee.
Churches are best for prayer, that have least light:
To see God only, I go out of sight:
 And to 'scape stormy days, I choose
  An everlasting night.

JOHN DONNE

The Night. John, III, 2

 Through that pure *Virgin-shrine*,
That sacred vail drawn o'r thy glorious noon
That men might look and live as Glo-worms shine,
  And face the Moon:
Wise *Nicodemus* saw such light
As made him know his God by night.

  Most blest believer he!
Who in that land of darkness and blinde eyes
Thy long expected healing wings could see,
  When thou didst rise,
And what can never more be done,
Did at mid-night speak with the Sun!

O who will tell me, where
He found thee at that dead and silent hour!
What hallow'd solitary ground did bear
    So rare a flower,
  Within whose sacred leafs did lie
  The fulness of the Deity.

  No mercy-seat of gold,
No dead and dusty *Cherub*, nor carv'd stone,
But his own living works did my Lord hold
    And lodge alone;
  Where *trees* and *herbs* did watch and peep
And wonder, while the *Jews* did sleep.

  Dear night! this worlds defeat;
The stop to busie fools; cares check and curb;
The day of Spirits; my souls calm retreat
    Which none disturb!
Christs progress, and his prayer time;
The hours to which high Heaven doth chime.

  Gods silent, searching flight:
When my Lords head is fill'd with dew, and all
His locks are wet with the clear drops of night;
    His still, soft call;
His knocking time; The souls dumb watch,
  When Spirits their fair kindred catch.

  Were all my loud, evil days
Calm and unhaunted as is thy dark Tent,
Whose peace but by some *Angels* wing or voice
    Is seldom rent;
  Then I in Heaven all the long year
  Would keep, and never wander here.

But living where the Sun
Doth all things wake, and where all mix and tyre
Themselves and others, I consent and run
    To ev'ry myre,
And by this worlds ill-guiding light,
Erre more than I can do by night.

    There is in God (some say)
A deep, but dazling darkness; As men here
Say it is late and dusky, because they
    See not all clear
O for that night! where I in him
Might live invisible and dim.

HENRY VAUGHAN

Prayer (I)

Prayer the Churches banquet, Angels age,
    Gods breath in man returning to his birth,
    The soul in paraphrase, heart in pilgrimage,
The Christian plummet sounding heav'n and earth;
Engine against th' Almightie, sinners towre,
    Reversed thunder, Christ-side-piercing spear,
    The six-daies world transposing in an houre,
A kinde of tune, which all things heare and fear;
Softnesse, and peace, and joy, and love, and blisse,
    Exalted Manna, gladnesse of the best,
    Heaven in ordinarie, man well drest,
The milkie way, the bird of Paradise,
    Church-bels beyond the starres heard, the souls bloud,
    The land of spices; something understood.

GEORGE HERBERT

Batter My Heart

Batter my heart, three-personed God; for, you
As yet but knock, breathe, shine, and seek to mend;
That I may rise, and stand, o'erthrow me, and bend
Your force, to break, blow, burn, and make me new.
I, like an usurped town, to another due,
Labour to admit you, but oh, to no end,
Reason your viceroy in me, me should defend,
But is captived, and proves weak or untrue,
Yet dearly'I love you, and would be loved fain,
But am betrothed unto your enemy,
Divorce me, untie, or break that knot again,
Take me to you, imprison me, for I
Except you enthral me, never shall be free,
Nor ever chaste, except you ravish me.

JOHN DONNE

From Samson Agonistes

Chorus   All is best, though we oft doubt,
What th' unsearchable dispose
Of highest wisdom brings about,
And ever best found in the close.
Oft he seems to hide his face,
But unexpectedly returns
And to his faithful Champion hath in place
Bore witness gloriously; whence *Gaza* mourns
And all that band them to resist
His uncontroulable intent,
His servants he with new acquist
Of true experience from this great event
With peace and consolation hath dismist,
And calm of mind all passion spent.

JOHN MILTON

Auguries of Innocence

To see a World in a Grain of Sand,
And a Heaven in a Wild Flower,
Hold Infinity in the palm of your hand,
And Eternity in an hour.

A Robin Redbreast in a cage
Puts all Heaven in a rage.
A dove-house fill'd with Doves and Pigeons
Shudders Hell thro' all its regions.
A Dog starv'd at his Master's gate
Predicts the ruin of the State.
A Horse misus'd upon the road
Calls to Heaven for Human blood.
Each outcry of the hunted Hare
A fibre from the Brain does tear.
A Skylark wounded in the wing,
A Cherubim does cease to sing.
The Game-Cock clipt and arm'd for fight
Does the Rising Sun affright.
Every Wolf's and Lion's howl
Raises from Hell a Human Soul.

The wild Deer, wandering here and there,
Keeps the Human Soul from care.
The Lamb misus'd breeds Public Strife,
And yet forgives the Butcher's knife.
He who shall hurt the little Wren
Shall never be belov'd by Men.
He who the Ox to wrath has mov'd
Shall never be by Woman lov'd.
The wanton Boy that kills the Fly
Shall feel the Spider's enmity.
He who torments the Chafer's Sprite
Weaves a Bower in endless Night.
The Catterpiller on the Leaf
Repeats to thee thy Mother's grief.

Kill not the Moth nor Butterfly,
For the Last Judgment draweth nigh.
He who shall train the Horse to war
Shall never pass the Polar Bar.
The Beggar's Dog and Widow's Cat,
Feed them, and thou wilt grow fat.

The Bat that flits at close of eve
Has left the Brain that won't believe.
The Owl that calls upon the night
Speaks the Unbeliever's fright.
The Gnat that sings his Summer's song
Poison gets from Slander's tongue.
The poison of the Snake and Newt
Is the sweat of Envy's foot.
The poison of the Honey Bee
Is the Artist's Jealousy.
A Truth that's told with bad intent
Beats all the Lies you can invent.

Joy and Woe are woven fine,
A Clothing for the Soul divine;
Under every grief and pine
Runs a Joy with silken twine.
It is right it should be so;
Man was made for Joy and Woe;
And when this we rightly know,
Thro' the World we safely go.
The Babe is more than Swadling-bands;
Throughout all these Human lands
Tools were made, and born were hands,
Every Farmer understands.
Every Tear from every Eye
Becomes a Babe in Eternity;
This is caught by Females bright,
And return'd to its own delight.
The Bleat, the Bark, Bellow, and Roar
Are Waves that beat on Heaven's Shore.

The Babe that weeps the Rod beneath
Writes Revenge in realms of Death.
He who mocks the Infant's Faith
Shall be mock'd in Age and Death.
He who shall teach the Child to doubt
The rotting Grave shall ne'er get out.
He who respects the Infant's Faith
Triumphs over Hell and Death.
The Child's Toys and the Old Man's Reasons
Are the Fruits of the Two Seasons.
The Questioner, who sits so sly,
Shall never know how to reply.
He who replies to words of Doubt
Doth put the Light of Knowledge out.
A Riddle, or the Cricket's cry,
Is to Doubt a fit Reply.
The Emmet's Inch and Eagle's Mile
Make lame Philosophy to smile.
He who doubts from what he sees
Will ne'er believe, do what you please.
If the Sun and Moon should doubt,
They'd immediately go out.

The Prince's Robes and Beggar's Rags
Are Toadstools on the Miser's Bags.
The Beggar's Rags, fluttering in air,
Does to Rags the Heavens tear.
The Poor Man's Farthing is worth more
Than all the Gold on Afric's shore.
One Mite wrung from the Lab'rer's hands
Shall buy and sell the Miser's lands;
Or, if protected from on high,
Does that whole Nation sell and buy.
The Soldier, arm'd with Sword and Gun,
Palsied strikes the Summer's Sun.
The strongest Poison ever known
Came from Caesar's Laurel Crown.
Nought can deform the Human Race

Like to the Armour's iron brace.
When Gold and Gems adorn the Plow
To peaceful Arts shall Envy bow.
To be in a Passion you Good may do,
But no Good if a Passion is in you.
The Whore and Gambler, by the State
Licensed, build that Nation's Fate.
The Harlot's cry from street to street
Shall weave Old England's winding-sheet.
The Winner's shout, the Loser's curse,
Dance before dead England's Hearse.

Every Night and every Morn
Some to Misery are born.
Every Morn and every Night
Some are born to Sweet Delight.
Some are born to Sweet Delight,
Some are born to Endless Night.
We are led to believe a Lie
When we see not thro' the Eye,
Which was born in a Night, to perish in a Night,
When the Soul slept in Beams of Light.
God appears, and God is Light,
To those poor Souls who dwell in Night;
But does a Human Form display
To those who dwell in Realms of Day.

WILLIAM BLAKE

From Paradise Lost (Book XII)

So spake our Mother *Eve*, and *Adam* heard
Well pleas'd, but answer'd not; for now too nigh
Th' Archangel stood, and from the other Hill
To thir fixt Station, all in bright array
The Cherubim descended; on the ground
Gliding meteorous, as Ev'ning Mist
Ris'n from a River o're the marish glides,
And gathers ground fast at the Labourers heel
Homeward returning. High in Front advanc't,
The brandisht Sword of God before them blaz'd
Fierce as a Comet; which with torrid heat,
And vapour as the *Libyan* Air adust,
Began to parch that temperate Clime; whereat
In either hand the hastning Angel caught
Our lingring Parents, and to th' Eastern Gate
Led them direct, and down the Cliff as fast
To the subjected Plaine; then disappeer'd.
They looking back, all th' Eastern side beheld
Of Paradise, so late thir happie seat,
Wav'd over by that flaming Brand, the Gate
With dreadful Faces throng'd and fierie Armes:
Som natural tears they drop'd, but wip'd them soon;
The World was all before them, where to choose
Thir place of rest, and Providence thir guide:
They hand in hand with wandring steps and slow,
Through *Eden* took thir solitarie way.

JOHN MILTON

A Hare

Eyes that glass fear, though fear on furtive foot
　　Track thee, in slumber bound;
Ears that whist danger, though the wind sigh not,
　　Nor Echo list a sound;
Heart—oh, what hazard must thy wild life be,
With sapient Man for thy cold enemy!

Fleet Scatterbrains, thou hast thine hours of peace
　　In pastures April-green,
Where the shrill skylark's raptures never cease,
And the clear dew englobes the white moon's beam.
All happiness God gave thee, albeit thy foe
Roves Eden, as did Satan, long ago.

WALTER DE LA MARE

From Paradise Lost (Book IX)

　　So spake the Enemie of Mankind, enclos'd
In Serpent, Inmate bad, and toward *Eve*
Address'd his way, not with indented wave,
Prone on the ground, as since, but on his reare,
Circular base of rising foulds, that tour'd
Fould above foul a surging Maze, his Head
Crested aloft, and Carbuncle his Eyes;
With burnisht Neck of verdant Gold, erect
Amidst his circling Spires, that on the grass
Floted redundant: pleasing was his shape,
And lovely, never since of Serpent kind
Lovelier, not those that in *Illyria* chang'd
Hermione and *Cadmus*, or the God
In *Epidaurus*; nor to which transformd
Ammonian Jove, or *Capitoline* was seen,
Hee with *Olympias*, this with her who bore

Scipio the highth of *Rome*. With tract oblique
At first, as one who sought access, but feard
To interrupt, side-long he works his way.
As when a Ship by skilful Stearsman wrought
Nigh Rivers mouth or Foreland, where the Wind
Veres oft, as oft so steers, and shifts her Saile;
So varied hee, and of his tortuous Traine
Curld many a wanton wreath in sight of *Eve*,
To lure her Eye; shee busied heard the sound
Of rusling Leaves, but minded not, as us'd
To such disport before her through the Field,
From every Beast, more duteous at her call,
Then at *Circean* call the Herd disguis'd.
Hee boulder now, uncall'd before her stood;
But as in gaze admiring: Oft he bowd
His turret Crest, and sleek enamel'd Neck,
Fawning, and lick'd the ground whereon she trod.
His gentle dumb expression turnd at length
The Eye of *Eve* to mark his play; he glad
Of her attention gaind, with Serpent Tongue
Organic, or impulse of vocal Air,
His fraudulent temptation thus began.

                                        JOHN MILTON

Never Again would Birds' Song be the Same

He would declare and could himself believe
That the birds there in all the garden round
From having heard the daylong voice of Eve
Had added to their own an oversound,
Her tone of meaning but without the words.
Admittedly an eloquence so soft
Could only have had an influence on birds
When call or laughter carried it aloft.
Be that as may be, she was in their song.
Moreover her voice upon their voices crossed
Had now persisted in the woods so long
That probably it never would be lost.
Never again would birds' song be the same.
And to do that to birds was why she came.

ROBERT FROST

The Aziola

I

'Do you not hear the Aziola cry?
        Methinks she must be nigh,'
    Said Mary, as we sate
In dusk, ere stars were lit, or candles brought;
        And I, who thought
    This Aziola was some tedious woman,
        Asked, 'Who is Aziola?' How elate
I felt to know that it was nothing human,
        No mockery of myself to fear or hate:
        And Mary saw my soul,
And laughed, and said, 'Disquiet yourself not;
        'Tis nothing but a little downy owl.'

II

Sad Aziola! many an eventide
    Thy music I had heard
By wood and stream, meadow and mountain-side,
    And fields and marshes wide,—
Such as nor voice, nor lute, nor wind, nor bird,
    The soul ever stirred;
Unlike and far sweeter than them all.
Sad Aziola! from that moment I
    Loved thee and thy sad cry.

PERCY BYSSHE SHELLEY

The Owl

Downhill I came, hungry, and yet not starved;
Cold, yet had heat within me that was proof
Against the North wind, tired, yet so that rest
Had seemed the sweetest thing under a roof.

Then at the inn I had food, fire, and rest,
Knowing how hungry, cold, and tired was I.
All of the night was quite barred out except
An owl's cry, a most melancholy cry

Shaken out long and clear upon the hill,
No merry note, nor cause of merriment,
But one telling me plain what I escaped
And others could not, that night, as in I went.

And salted was my food, and my repose,
Salted and sobered, too, by the bird's voice
Speaking for all who lay under the stars,
Soldiers and poor, unable to rejoice.

EDWARD THOMAS

The Kraken

Below the thunders of the upper deep;
Far, far beneath in the abysmal sea,
His ancient, dreamless, uninvaded sleep
The Kraken sleepeth: faintest sunlights flee
About his shadowy sides: above him swell
Huge sponges of millennial growth and height;
And far away into the sickly light,
From many a wondrous grot and secret cell
Unnumbered and enormous polypi
Winnow with giant arms the slumbering green.
There hath he lain for ages and will lie
Battening upon huge seaworms in his sleep,
Until the latter fire shall heat the deep;
Then once by man and angels to be seen,
In roaring he shall rise and on the surface die.

ALFRED, LORD TENNYSON

The World Below the Brine

The world below the brine,
Forests at the bottom of the sea, the branches and leaves,
Sea-lettuce, vast lichens, strange flowers and seeds, the
  thick tangle, openings, and pink turf,
Different colors, pale gray and green, purple, white, and
  gold, the play of light through the water,
Dumb swimmers there among the rocks, coral, gluten,
  grass, rushes, and the aliment of the swimmers,
Sluggish existences grazing there suspended, or slowly
  crawling close to the bottom,
The sperm-whale at the surface blowing air and spray, or
  disporting with his flukes,
The leaden-eyed shark, the walrus, the turtle, the hairy
  sea-leopard, and the sting-ray,
Passions there, wars, pursuits, tribes, sight in those ocean-
  depths, breathing that thick-breathing air, as so
  many do,
The change thence to the sight here, and to the subtle air
  breathed by beings like us who walk this sphere,
The change onward from ours to that of beings who walk
  other spheres.

WALT WHITMAN

From Paradise Lost (Book I)

Whereto with speedy words th' Arch-fiend reply'd.
 Fall'n Cherube, to be weak is miserable
Doing or Suffering: but of this be sure,
To do ought good never will be our task,
But ever to do ill our sole delight,
As being the contrary to his high will
Whom we resist. If then his Providence
Out of our evil seek to bring forth good,
Our labour must be to pervert that end,

And out of good still to find means of evil;
Which oft times may succeed, so as perhaps
Shall grieve him, if I fail not, and disturb
His inmost counsels from their destind aim.
But see the angry Victor hath recall'd
His Ministers of vengeance and pursuit
Back to the Gates of Heav'n: The Sulphurous Hail
Shot after us in storm, oreblown hath laid
The fiery Surge, that from the Precipice
Of Heav'n receiv'd us falling, and the Thunder,
Wing'd with red Lightning and impetuous rage,
Perhaps hath spent his shafts, and ceases now
To bellow through the vast and boundless Deep.
Let us not slip th' occasion, whether scorn,
Or satiate fury yield it from our Foe.
Seest thou yon dreary Plain, forlorn and wilde,
The seat of desolation, voyd of light,
Save what the glimmering of these livid flames
Casts pale and dreadful? Thither let us tend
From off the tossing of these fiery waves,
There rest, if any rest can harbour there,
And reassembling our afflicted Powers,
Consult how we may henceforth most offend
Our Enemy, our own loss how repair,
How overcome this dire Calamity,
What reinforcement we may gain from Hope,
If not what resolution from despare.
    Thus Satan talking to his neerest Mate
With Head up-lift above the wave, and Eyes
That sparkling blaz'd, his other Parts besides
Prone on the Flood, extended long and large
Lay floating many a rood, in bulk as huge
As whom the Fables name of monstrous size,
Titanian, or *Earth-born*, that warr'd on *Jove*,
Briarios or *Typhon*, whom the Den
By ancient *Tarsus* held, or that Sea-beast
Leviathan, which God of all his works
Created hugest that swim th' Ocean stream:

Him haply slumbring on the *Norway* foam
The Pilot of some small night-founder'd Skiff,
Deeming some Island, oft, as Sea-men tell,
With fixed Anchor in his skaly rind
Moors by his side under the Lee, while Night
Invests the Sea, and wished Morn delayes:
So stretcht out huge in length the Arch-fiend lay
Chain'd on the burning Lake . . .

JOHN MILTON

From Paradise Lost (Book II)

Another part in Squadrons and gross Bands,
On bold adventure to discover wide
That dismal world, if any Clime perhaps
Might yeild them easier habitation, bend
Four ways thir flying March, along the Banks
Of four infernal Rivers that disgorge
Into the burning Lake thir baleful streams;
Abhorred *Styx* the flood of deadly hate,
Sad *Acheron* of sorrow, black and deep;
Cocytus, nam'd of lamentation loud
Heard on the ruful stream; fierce *Phlegeton*
Whose waves of torrent fire inflame with rage.
Farr off from these a slow and silent stream,
Lethe the River of Oblivion roules
Her watrie Labyrinth, whereof who drinks,
Forthwith his former state and being forgets,
Forgets both joy and grief, pleasure and pain.
Beyond this flood a frozen Continent
Lies dark and wilde, beat with perpetual storms
Of Whirlwind and dire Hail, which on firm land
Thaws not, but gathers heap, and ruin seems
Of ancient pile; all else deep snow and ice,
A gulf profound as that *Serbonian* Bog

Betwixt *Damiata* and mount *Casius* old,
Where Armies whole have sunk: the parching Air
Burns frore, and cold performs th' effect of Fire.
Thither by harpy-footed Furies hail'd,
At certain revolutions all the damn'd
Are brought: and feel by turns the bitter change
Of fierce extreams, extreams by change more fierce,
From Beds of raging Fire to starve in Ice
Thir soft Ethereal warmth, and there to pine
Immovable, infixt, and frozen round,
Periods of time, thence hurried back to fire.
They ferry over this *Lethean* Sound
Both to and fro, thir sorrow to augment,
And wish and struggle, as they pass, to reach
The tempting stream, with one small drop to loose
In sweet forgetfulness all pain and woe,
All in one moment, and so neer the brink;
But fate withstands, and to oppose th' attempt
Medusa with *Gorgonian* terror guards
The Ford, and of it self the water flies
All taste of living wight, as once it fled
The lip of *Tantalus*. Thus roving on
In confus'd march forlorn, th' adventrous Bands
With shuddring horror pale, and eyes agast
View'd first thir lamentable lot, and found
No rest: through many a dark and drearie Vaile
They pass'd, and many a Region dolorous,
O're many a Frozen, many a Fierie Alpe,
Rocks, Caves, Lakes, Fens, Bogs, Dens, and shades of death,
A Universe of death, which God by curse
Created evil, for evil only good,
Where all life dies, death lives, and nature breeds,
Perverse, all monstrous, all prodigious things,
Abominable, inutterable, and worse
Then Fables yet have feign'd, or fear conceiv'd,
Gorgons and *Hydra's*, and *Chimera's* dire.

JOHN MILTON

The Tempest (Act III, sc ii)

CALIBAN: Art thou afeard?
STEPHANO: No, monster, not I.
CALIBAN: Be not afeard. The isle is full of noises,
Sounds, and sweet airs, that give delight, and hurt not.
Sometimes a thousand twangling instruments
Will hum about mine ears; and sometime voices,
That, if I then had wak'd after long sleep,
Will make me sleep again; and then, in dreaming,
The clouds methought would open and show riches
Ready to drop upon me, that, when I wak'd,
I cried to dream again.

WILLIAM SHAKESPEARE

The Cutty Wren

O where are you going? says Milder to Melder,
O where are you going? says the younger to the elder.
O I cannot tell, says Festel to Fose.
We're going to the woods, said John the Red Nose,
We're going to the woods, said John the Red Nose.

O what will you do there? says Milder to Melder,
O what will you do there? says the younger to the elder.
O I cannot tell, says Festel to Fose.
To shoot the cutty wren, said John the Red Nose,
To shoot the cutty wren, said John the Red Nose.

O what will you shoot her with? says Milder to Melder,
O what will you shoot her with? says the younger to the
    elder.
Oh I cannot tell, says Festel to Fose.
With bows and with arrows, said John the Red Nose,
With bows and with arrows, said John the Red Nose.

O that will not do, says Milder to Melder,
O that will not do, says the younger to the elder.
O what will do then? says Festel to Fose.
With great guns and cannons, said John the Red Nose,
With great guns and cannons, said John the Red Nose.

O what will you bring her home in? says Milder to Melder,
O what will you bring her home in? says the younger to the
     elder.
O I cannot tell, says Festel to Fose.
On four strong men's shoulders, said John the Red Nose,
On four strong men's shoulders, said John the Red Nose.

O that will not do, says Milder to Melder,
O that will not do, says the younger to the elder.
O what will do then? says Festel to Fose.
On big carts and waggons, said John the Red Nose,
On big carts and waggons, said John the Red Nose.

What will you cut her up with? says Milder to Melder,
What will you cut her up with? says the younger to the
     elder.
O I do not know, says Festel to Fose.
With knives and with forks, said John the Red Nose,
With knives and with forks, said John the Red Nose.

O that will not do, says Milder to Melder,
O that will not do, says the younger to the elder.
O what will do then? says Festel to Fose.
With hatchets and cleavers, said John the Red Nose,
With hatchets and cleavers, said John the Red Nose.

What will you boil her in? says Milder to Melder,
What will you boil her in? says the younger to the elder.
Oh I cannot tell, says Festel to Fose.
In pots and in kettles, said John the Red Nose,
In pots and in kettles, said John the Red Nose.

O that will not do, says Milder to Melder,
O that will not do, says the younger to the elder.
O what will do then? says Festel to Fose.
In brass pans and cauldrons, said John the Red Nose,
In brass pans and cauldrons, said John the Red Nose.

ANON

Epilogue to 'The Orators'

'O where are you going?' said reader to rider,
'That valley is fatal when furnaces burn,
Yonder's the midden whose odours will madden,
That gap is the grave where the tall return.'

'O do you imagine,' said fearer to farer,
'That dusk will delay on your path to the pass,
Your diligent looking discover the lacking
Your footsteps feel from granite to grass?'

'O what was that bird,' said horror to hearer,
'Did you see that shape in the twisted trees?
Behind you swiftly the figure comes softly,
The spot on your skin is a shocking disease?'

'Out of this house'—said rider to reader
'Yours never will'—said farer to fearer
'They're looking for you'—said hearer to horror
As he left them there, as he left them there.

W. H. AUDEN

Low Barometer

The south-wind strengthens to a gale,
Across the moon the clouds fly fast,
The house is smitten as with a flail,
The chimney shudders to the blast.

On such a night, when Air has loosed
Its guardian grasp on blood and brain,
Old terrors then of god or ghost
Creep from their caves to life again;

And Reason kens he herits in
A haunted house. Tenants unknown
Assert their squalid lease of sin
With earlier title than his own.

Unbodied presences, the pack'd
Pollution and remorse of Time,
Slipp'd from oblivion reenact
The horrors of unhouseld crime.

Some men would quell the thing with prayer
Whose sightless footsteps pad the floor,
Whose fearful trespass mounts the stair
Or bursts the lock's forbidden door.

Some have seen corpses long interr'd
Escape from hallowing control,
Pale charnel forms—nay ev'n have heard
The shrilling of a troubled soul,

That wanders till the dawn hath cross'd
The dolorous dark, or Earth hath wound
Closer her storm-spredd cloke, and thrust
The baleful phantoms underground.

ROBERT BRIDGES

The Tempest (Act IV, sc i)

PROSPERO: You do look, my son, in a mov'd sort,
As if you were dismay'd; be cheerful, sir.
Our revels now are ended. These our actors,
As I foretold you, were all spirits, and
Are melted into air, into thin air;
And, like the baseless fabric of this vision,
The cloud-capp'd towers, the gorgeous palaces,
The solemn temples, the great globe itself,
Yea, all which it inherit, shall dissolve,
And, like this insubstantial pageant faded,
Leave not a rack behind. We are such stuff
As dreams are made on; and our little life
Is rounded with a sleep. Sir I am vex'd;
Bear with my weakness; my old brain is troubled;
Be not disturb'd with my infirmity.
If you be pleas'd, retire into my cell
And there repose; a turn or two I'll walk
To still my beating mind.

WILLIAM SHAKESPEARE

Henry V (Act IV, Prologue)

CHORUS: Now entertain conjecture of a time
When creeping murmur and the poring dark
Fills the wide vessel of the universe.
From camp to camp, through the foul womb of night,
The hum of either army stilly sounds,
That the fix'd sentinels almost receive
The secret whispers of each other's watch.
Fire answers fire, and through their paly flames
Each battle sees the other's umber'd face;
Steed threatens steed, in high and boastful neighs
Piercing the night's dull ear; and from the tents

The armourers accomplishing the knights,
With busy hammers closing rivets up,
Give dreadful note of preparation.
The country cocks do crow, the clocks do toll,
And the third hour of drowsy morning name.
Proud of their numbers and secure in soul,
The confident and over-lusty French
Do the low-rated English play at dice;
And chide the cripple tardy-gaited night
Who like a foul and ugly witch doth limp
So tediously away. The poor condemned English,
Like sacrifices, by their watchful fires
Sit patiently and inly ruminate
The morning's danger; and their gesture sad
Investing lank-lean cheeks and war-worn coats
Presenteth them unto the gazing moon
So many horrid ghosts. O, now, who will behold
The royal captain of this ruin'd band
Walking from watch to watch, from tent to tent,
Let him cry 'Praise and glory on his head!'
For forth he goes and visits all his host;
Bids them good morrow with a modest smile,
And calls them brothers, friends, and countrymen.
Upon his royal face there is no note
How dread an army hath enrounded him;
Nor doth he dedicate one jot of colour
Unto the weary and all-watched night;
But freshly looks, and over-bears attaint
With cheerful semblance and sweet majesty;
That every wretch, pining and pale before,
Beholding him, plucks comfort from his looks;
A largess universal, like the sun,
His liberal eye doth give to every one,

Thawing cold fear, that mean and gentle all
Behold, as may unworthiness define,
A little touch of Harry in the night.
And so our scene must to the battle fly:
Where—O for pity!—we shall much disgrace
With four or five most vile and ragged foils,
Right ill-dispos'd in brawl ridiculous,
The name of Agincourt. . . .

WILLIAM SHAKESPEARE

Antony and Cleopatra (Act I, sc iv)

CAESAR: Antony,
Leave thy lascivious wassails. When thou once
Was beaten from Modena, where thou slew'st
Hirtius and Pansa, consuls, at thy heel
Did famine follow; whom thou fought'st against,
Though daintily brought up, with patience more
Than savages could suffer. Thou didst drink
The stale of horses and the gilded puddle
Which beasts would cough at. Thy palate then did deign
The roughest berry on the rudest hedge;
Yea, like the stag when snow the pasture sheets,
The barks of trees thou brows'd. On the Alps
It is reported thou didst eat strange flesh
Which some did die to look on. And all this—
It wounds thine honour that I speak it now—
Was borne so like a soldier that thy cheek
So much as lank'd not.

WILLIAM SHAKESPEARE

Henry IV, Part I (Act IV, sc ii)

FALSTAFF: If I be not ashamed of my soldiers, I am a
sous'd gurnet. I have misused the King's press damnably.
I have got, in exchange of a hundred and fifty soldiers,
three hundred and odd pounds. I press me none but good
householders, yeomen's sons; inquire me out contracted
bachelors, such as had been ask'd twice on the banns; such
a commodity of warm slaves as had as lief hear the devil as
a drum; such as fear the report of a caliver worse than a
struck fowl or a hurt wild-duck. I press'd me none but
such toasts-and-butter, with hearts in their bellies no bigger
than pins' heads, and they have bought out their services;
and now my whole charge consists of ancients, corporals,
lieutenants, gentlemen of companies—slaves as ragged as
Lazarus in the painted cloth, where the Glutton's dogs
licked his sores; and such as indeed were never soldiers,
but discarded unjust servingmen, younger sons to younger
brothers, revolted tapsters, and ostlers trade-fall'n; the
cankers of a calm world and a long peace; ten times more
dishonourable ragged than an old-fac'd ancient. And such
have I, to fill up the rooms of them as have bought out
their services, that you would think that I had a hundred
and fifty tattered Prodigals lately come from swinekeeping,
from eating draff and husks. A mad fellow met me on the
way, and told me I had unloaded all the gibbets and
press'd the dead bodies. No eye hath seen such scarecrows.
I'll not march through Coventry with them, that's flat.
Nay, and the villains march wide betwixt the legs, as if
they had gyves on; for indeed I had the most of them out
of prison. There's not a shirt and a half in all my company;
and the half shirt is two napkins tack'd together and
thrown over the shoulders like a herald's coat without
sleeves; and the shirt, to say the truth, stol'n from my
host at Saint Albans, or the red-nose innkeeper of
Daventry. But that's all one; they'll find linen enough on
every hedge.

WILLIAM SHAKESPEARE

Stanzas

When a man hath no freedom to fight for at home,
    Let him combat for that of his neighbours;
Let him think of the glories of Greece and of Rome,
    And get knock'd on the head for his labours.
To do good to mankind is the chivalrous plan,
    And is always as nobly requited;
Then battle for freedom wherever you can,
    And, if not shot or hang'd, you'll get knighted.

LORD BYRON

Dawn Bombardment

Guns from the sea open against us:
The smoke rocks bodily in the casemate
And a yell of doom goes up.
We count and bless each new, heavy concussion –
Captives awaiting rescue.

Visiting angel of the wild-fire hair
Who in dream reassured us nightly
Where we lay fettered,
Laugh at us, as we wake – our faces
So tense with hope the tears run down.

ROBERT GRAVES

The Roads Also

The roads also have their wistful rest,
When the weathercocks perch still and roost,
And the town is quiet like a candle-lit room—
The streets also dream their dream.

The old houses muse of the old days
And their fond trees leaning on them doze,
On their steps chatter and clatter stops,
On their doors a strange hand taps.

Men remember alien ardours
As the dusk unearths old mournful odours.
In the garden unborn child souls wail
And the dead scribble on walls.

Though their own child cry for them in tears,
Women weep but hear no sound upstairs.
They believe in loves they had not lived
And in passion past the reach of the stairs
    To the world's towers or stars.

WILFRED OWEN

Gone, Gone Again

Gone, gone again,
May, June, July,
And August gone,
Again gone by,

Not memorable
Save that I saw them go,
As past the empty quays
The rivers flow.

And now again,
In the harvest rain,
The Blenheim oranges
Fall grubby from the trees

As when I was young—
And when the lost one was here—
And when the war began
To turn young men to dung.

Look at the old house,
Outmoded, dignified,
Dark and untenanted,
With grass growing instead

Of the footsteps of life,
The friendliness, the strife;
In its beds have lain
Youth, love, age, and pain:

I am something like that;
Only I am not dead,
Still breathing and interested
In the house that is not dark:—

I am something like that:
Not one pane to reflect the sun,
For the schoolboys to throw at—
They have broken every one.

EDWARD THOMAS

To a Friend Whose Work has Come to Nothing

Now all the truth is out,
Be secret and take defeat
From any brazen throat,
For how can you compete,
Being honour bred, with one
Who, were it proved he lies,
Were neither shamed in his own
Nor in his neighbours' eyes?
Bred to a harder thing
Than Triumph, turn away
And like a laughing string
Whereon mad fingers play
Amid a place of stone,
Be secret and exult,
Because of all things known
That is most difficult.

W. B. YEATS

Pericles, Prince of Tyre (Act III, sc i)

PERICLES: A terrible childbed hast thou had, my dear;
No light, no fire. Th' unfriendly elements
Forgot thee utterly; nor have I time
To give thee hallow'd to thy grave, but straight
Must cast thee, scarcely coffin'd, in the ooze;
Where, for a monument upon thy bones,
And aye-remaining lamps, the belching whale
And humming water must o'erwhelm thy corpse,
Lying with simple shells.

WILLIAM SHAKESPEARE

Mary Suffers with Her Son

Why have ye no reuthe on my child?
Have reuthe on me, full of murning.
Taket down on Rode my derworthy child,
Or prek me on Rode with my derling.

More pine ne may me ben don
Than laten me liven in sorwe and shame.
Als love me bindet to my sone,
So lat us deiyen bothen isame.

ANON (mid-14th century)

The Toys

My little Son, who looked from thoughtful eyes
And moved and spoke in quiet grown-up wise,
Having my law the seventh time disobeyed,
I struck him, and dismissed
With hard words and unkissed,
His Mother, who was patient, being dead.
Then, fearing lest his grief should hinder sleep,
I visited his bed,
But found him slumbering deep,
With darkened eyelids, and their lashes yet
From his late sobbing wet.
And I, with moan,
Kissing away his tears, left others of my own;
For, on a table drawn beside his head,
He had put, within his reach,
A box of counters and a red-veined stone,
A piece of glass abraded by the beach,
And six or seven shells,
A bottle with bluebells
And two French copper coins, ranged there with careful art,
To comfort his sad heart.

So when that night I prayed
To God, I wept, and said:
Ah, when at last we lie with trancèd breath,
Not vexing Thee in death,
And Thou rememberest of what toys
We made our joys,
How weakly understood,
Thy great commanded good,
Then, fatherly not less
Than I whom Thou hast moulded from the clay,
Thou'lt leave Thy wrath, and say,
'I will be sorry for their childishness.'

COVENTRY PATMORE

A Prayer for My Son

Bid a strong ghost stand at the head
That my Michael may sleep sound,
Nor cry, nor turn in the bed
Till his morning meal come round;
And may departing twilight keep
All dread afar till morning's back,
That his mother may not lack
Her fill of sleep.

Bid the ghost have sword in fist:
Some there are, for I avow
Such devilish things exist,
Who have planned his murder, for they know
Of some most haughty deed or thought
That waits upon his future days,
And would through hatred of the bays
Bring that to nought.

Though You can fashion everything
From nothing every day, and teach
The morning stars to sing,
You have lacked articulate speech
To tell Your simplest want, and known,
Wailing upon a woman's knee,
All of that worst ignominy
Of flesh and bone;

And when through all the town there ran
The servants of Your enemy,
A woman and a man,
Unless the Holy writings lie,
Hurried through the smooth and rough
And through the fertile and waste,
Protecting, till the danger past,
With human love.

W. B. YEATS

On My First Sonne

Farewell, thou child of my right hand, and joy;
    My sinne was too much hope of thee, lov'd boy,
Seven yeeres tho'wert lent to me, and I thee pay,
    Exacted by thy fate, on the just day.
O, could I loose all father now. For why
    Will man lament the state he should envie?
To have so soone scap'd worlds, and fleshes rage,
    And, if no other miserie, yet age?
Rest in soft peace, and, ask'd, say here doth lye
    Ben. Jonson his best piece of *poetrie*.
For whose sake, hence-forth, all his vowes be such,
    As what he loves may never like too much.

BEN JONSON

The Two April Mornings

We walked along, while bright and red
Uprose the morning sun;
And Matthew stopped, he looked, and said,
"The will of God be done!"

A village schoolmaster was he,
With hair of glittering grey;
As blithe a man as you could see
On a spring holiday.

And on that morning, through the grass,
And by the steaming rills,
We travelled merrily, to pass
A day among the hills.

"Our work," said I, "was well begun,
Then from thy breast what thought,
Beneath so beautiful a sun,
So sad a sigh has brought?"

A second time did Matthew stop;
And fixing still his eye
Upon the eastern mountain-top,
To me he made reply:

"Yon cloud with that long purple cleft
Brings fresh into my mind
A day like this which I have left
Full thirty years behind.

"And just above yon slope of corn
Such colours, and no other,
Were in the sky, that April morn,
Of this the very brother.

"With rod and line I sued the sport
Which that sweet season gave,
And, to the churchyard come, stopped short
Beside my daughter's grave.

"Nine summers had she scarcely seen,
The pride of all the vale;
And then she sang;—she would have been
A very nightingale.

"Six feet in earth my Emma lay;
And yet I loved her more,
For so it seemed, than till that day
I e'er had loved before.

"And turning from her grave, I met
Beside the churchyard yew,
A blooming Girl, whose hair was wet
With points of morning dew.

"A basket on her head she bare;
Her brow was smooth and white:
To see a child so very fair,
It was a pure delight!

"No fountain from its rocky cave
E'er tripped with foot so free;
She seemed as happy as a wave
That dances on the sea.

"There came from me a sigh of pain
Which I could ill confine;
I looked at her, and looked again:
And did not wish her mine!"

Matthew is in his grave, yet now,
Methinks, I see him stand,
As at that moment, with a bough
Of wilding in his hand.

WILLIAM WORDSWORTH

A letter

A letter on a dusky wet morning:
to live after us like the smell of rooms,
or like the traditional way robins sing:
so children's manners are candlelight to tombs.
I say a marble head, a snowy rock,
will create space in the surrounding air:
poor masterpiece of light personal shock:,
but love never dies out, it is despair.
It lives more than the shape and smell of rooms,
persisting in manners as robins sing,
it is our children, carries light in tombs,
it is the coldest dawn, the clear morning.

PETER LEVI

Cymbeline (Act IV, sc ii)

ARVIRAGUS: With fairest flowers,
Whilst summer lasts and I live here, Fidele,
I'll sweeten thy sad grave. Thou shalt not lack
The flower that's like thy face, pale primrose; nor
The azur'd hare-bell, like thy veins; no nor
The leaf of eglantine, whom not to slander,
Out-sweet'ned not thy breath. The ruddock would,
With charitable bill—O bill, sore shaming
Those rich-left heirs that let their fathers lie
Without a monument!—bring thee all this;
Yea, and furr'd moss besides, when flow'rs are none,
To winter-ground thy corse.

WILLIAM SHAKESPEARE

A Refusal to Mourn the Death, by Fire, of a Child in London

Never until the mankind making
Bird beast and flower
Fathering and all humbling darkness
Tells with silence the last light breaking
And the still hour
Is come of the sea tumbling in harness

And I must enter again the round
Zion of the water bead
And the synagogue of the ear of corn
Shall I let pray the shadow of a sound
Or sow my salt seed
In the least valley of sackcloth to mourn

The majesty and burning of the child's death.
I shall not murder
The mankind of her going with a grave truth
Nor blaspheme down the stations of the breath
With any further
Elegy of innocence and youth.

Deep with the first dead lies London's daughter,
Robed in the long friends,
The grains beyond age, the dark veins of her mother,
Secret by the unmourning water
Of the riding Thames.
After the first death, there is no other.

DYLAN THOMAS

May with its Light Behaving

May with its light behaving
Stirs vessel, eye, and limb;
The singular and sad
Are willing to recover,
And to the swan-delighting river
The careless picnics come,
The living white and red.

The dead remote and hooded
In their enclosures rest; but we
From the vague woods have broken,
Forests where children meet
And the white angel-vampires flit;
We stand with shaded eye,
The dangerous apple taken.

The real world lies before us;
Animal motions of the young,
The common wish for death,
The pleasured and the haunted;
The dying master sinks tormented
In the admirers' ring,
The unjust walk the earth.

And love that makes impatient
The tortoise and the roe, and lays
The blonde beside the dark,
Urges upon our blood,
Before the evil and the good
How insufficient is
The endearment and the look.

W. H. AUDEN

Lycidas

In this Monody the Author bewails a learned Friend,
unfortunatly drown'd in his Passage from *Chester* on
the *Irish* Seas, 1637. And by occasion foretels the ruine
of our corrupted Clergy then in their height.

Yet once more, O ye Laurels, and once more
Ye Myrtles brown, with Ivy never-sear,
I com to pluck your Berries harsh and crude,
And with forc'd fingers rude,
Shatter your leaves before the mellowing year.
Bitter constraint, and sad occasion dear,
Compels me to disturb your season due:
For *Lycidas* is dead, dead ere his prime
Young *Lycidas*, and hath not left his peer:
Who would not sing for *Lycidas*? he knew
Himself to sing, and build the lofty rhyme.
He must not flote upon his watry bear
Unwept, and welter to the parching wind,
Without the meed of som melodious tear.
　　Begin then, Sisters of the sacred well,
That from beneath the seat of *Jove* doth spring,
Begin, and somwhat loudly sweep the string.
Hence with denial vain, and coy excuse,
So may som gentle Muse
With lucky words favour my destin'd Urn,
And as he passes turn,
And bid fair peace be to my sable shrowd.
For we were nurst upon the self-same hill,
Fed the same flock, by fountain, shade, and rill.
　　Together both, ere the high Lawns appear'd
Under the opening eye-lids of the morn,
We drove a field, and both together heard
What time the Gray-fly winds her sultry horn,
Batt'ning our flocks with the fresh dews of night,
Oft till the Star that rose, at Ev'ning, bright
Toward Heav'ns descent had slop'd his westering wheel.

Mean while the Rural ditties were not mute,
Temper'd to th'Oaten Flute,
Rough *Satyrs* danc'd, and *Fauns* with clov'n heel,
From the glad sound would not be absent long,
And old *Damætas* lov'd to hear our song.

But O the heavy change, now thou art gon,
Now thou art gon, and never must return!
Thee Shepherd, thee the Woods, and desert Caves,
With wilde Thyme and the gadding Vine o'regrown,
And all their echoes mourn.
The Willows, and the Hazle Copses green,
Shall now no more be seen,
Fanning their joyous Leaves to thy soft layes.
As killing as the Canker to the Rose,
Or Taint-worm to the weanling Herds that graze,
Or Frost to Flowers, that their gay wardrop wear,
When first the White thorn blows;
Such, *Lycidas*, thy loss to Shepherds ear.

Where were ye Nymphs when the remorseless deep
Clos'd o're the head of your lov'd *Lycidas*?
For neither were ye playing on the steep,
Where your old *Bards*, the famous *Druids* ly,
Nor on the shaggy top of *Mona* high,
Nor yet where *Deva* spreads her wisard stream:
Ay me, I fondly dream!
Had ye bin there . . for what could that have don?
What could the Muse her self that *Orpheus* bore,
The Muse her self, for her inchanting son
Whom Universal nature did lament,
When by the rout that made the hideous roar,
His goary visage down the stream was sent,
Down the swift *Hebrus* to the *Lesbian* shore.

Alas! What boots it with uncessant care
To tend the homely slighted Shepherds trade,
And strictly meditate the thankles Muse,
Were it not better don as others use,
To sport with *Amaryllis* in the shade,
Or with the tangles of *Neæra's* hair?

Fame is the spur that the clear spirit doth raise
(That last infirmity of Noble mind)
To scorn delights, and live laborious dayes;
But the fair Guerdon when we hope to find,
And think to burst out into sudden blaze,
Comes the blind *Fury* with th'abhorred shears,
And slits the thin spun life. But not the praise,
Phœbus repli'd, and touch'd my trembling ears;
Fame is no plant that grows on mortal soil,
Nor in the glistering foil
Set off to th'world, nor in broad rumour lies,
But lives and spreds aloft by those pure eyes,
And perfet witnes of all judging *Jove;*
As he pronounces lastly on each deed,
Of so much fame in Heav'n expect thy meed.
  O Fountain *Arethuse*, and thou honour'd floud,
Smooth-sliding *Mincius*, crown'd with vocall reeds,
That strain I heard was of a higher mood:
But now my Oate proceeds,
And listens to the Herald of the Sea
That came in *Neptune's* plea,
He ask'd the Waves, and ask'd the Fellon winds,
What hard mishap hath doom'd this gentle swain?
And question'd every gust of rugged wings
That blows from off each beaked Promontory,
They knew not of his story,
And sage *Hippotades* their answer brings,
That not a blast was from his dungeon stray'd,
The Ayr was calm, and on the level brine,
Sleek *Panope* with all her sisters play'd.
It was that fatall and perfidious Bark
Built in th'eclipse, and rigg'd with curses dark,
That sunk so low that sacred head of thine.
  Next *Camus*, reverend Sire, went footing slow,
His Mantle hairy, and his Bonnet sedge,
Inwrought with figures dim, and on the edge
Like to that sanguine flower inscrib'd with woe.
Ah! Who hath reft (quoth he) my dearest pledge?

Last came, and last did go,
The Pilot of the *Galilean* lake,
Two massy Keyes he bore of metals twain,
(The Golden opes, the Iron shuts amain)
He shook his Miter'd locks, and stern bespake,
How well could I have spar'd for thee young swain,
Anow of such as for their bellies sake,
Creep and intrude, and climb into the fold?
Of other care they little reck'ning make,
Then how to scramble at the shearers feast,
And shove away the worthy bidden guest.
Blind mouthes! that scarce themselves know how to hold
A Sheep-hook, or have learn'd ought els the least
That to the faithfull Herdmans art belongs!
What recks it them? What need they? They are sped;
And when they list, their lean and flashy songs
Grate on their scrannel Pipes of wretched straw,
The hungry Sheep look up, and are not fed,
But swoln with wind, and the rank mist they draw,
Rot inwardly, and foul contagion spread:
Besides what the grim Woolf with privy paw
Daily devours apace, and nothing sed,
But that two-handed engine at the door,
Stands ready to smite once, and smite no more.
   Return *Alpheus*, the dread voice is past,
That shrunk thy streams; Return *Sicilian* Muse,
And call the Vales, and bid them hither cast
Their Bels, and Flourets of a thousand hues.
Ye valleys low where the milde whispers use,
Of shades and wanton winds, and gushing brooks,
On whose fresh lap the swart Star sparely looks,
Throw hither all your quaint enameld eyes,
That on the green terf suck the honied showres,
And purple all the ground with vernal flowres.
Bring the rathe Primrose that forsaken dies.
The tufted Crow-toe, and pale Gessamine,
The white Pink, and the Pansie freakt with jeat,
The glowing Violet.

The Musk-rose, and the well attir'd Woodbine,
With Cowslips wan that hang the pensive hed,
And every flower that sad embroidery wears:
Bid *Amaranthus* all his beauty shed,
And Daffadillies fill their cups with tears,
To strew the Laureat Herse where *Lycid* lies.
For so to interpose a little ease,
Let our frail thoughts dally with false surmise.
Ay me! Whilst thee the shores, and sounding Seas
Wash far away, where ere thy bones are hurld,
Whether beyond the stormy *Hebrides*,
Where thou perhaps under the whelming tide
Visit'st the bottom of the monstrous world;
Or whether thou to our moist vows deny'd,
Sleep'st by the fable of *Bellerus* old,
Where the great vision of the guarded Mount
Looks toward *Namancos* and *Bayona's* hold;
Look homeward Angel now, and melt with ruth.
And, O ye *Dolphins*, waft the haples youth.
    Weep no more, woful Shepherds weep no more,
For *Lycidas* your sorrow is not dead,
Sunk though he be beneath the watry floar,
So sinks the day-star in the Ocean bed,
And yet anon repairs his drooping head,
And tricks his beams, and with new spangled Ore,
Flames in the forehead of the morning sky:
So *Lycidas* sunk low, but mounted high,
Through the dear might of him that walk'd the waves
Where other groves, and other streams along,
With *Nectar* pure his oozy Lock's he laves,
And hears the unexpressive nuptiall Song,
In the blest Kingdoms meek of joy and love.
There entertain him all the Saints above,
In solemn troops, and sweet Societies
That sing, and singing in their glory move,
And wipe the tears for ever from his eyes.
Now *Lycidas* the Shepherds weep no more;

Hence forth thou art the Genius of the shore,
In thy large recompense, and shalt be good
To all that wander in that perilous flood.
   Thus sang the uncouth Swain to th'Okes and rills,
While the still morn went out with Sandals gray,
He touch'd the tender stops of various Quills,
With eager thought warbling his *Dorick* lay:
And now the Sun had stretch'd out all the hills,
And now was dropt into the Western bay;
At last he rose, and twitch'd his Mantle blew:
To morrow to fresh Woods, and Pastures new.

JOHN MILTON

In honour of
St. Alphonsus Rodriguez

Laybrother of the Society of Jesus

Honour is flashed off exploit, so we say;
And those strokes once that gashed flesh or galled shield
Should tongue that time now, trumpet now that field,
And, on the fighter, forge his glorious day.
On Christ they do and on the martyr may;
But be the war within, the brand we wield
Unseen, the heroic breast not outward-steeled,
Earth hears no hurtle then from fiercest fray.

   Yet God (that hews mountain and continent,
Earth, all, out; who, with trickling increment,
Veins violets and tall trees makes more and more)
Could crowd career with conquest while there went
Those years and years by of world without event
That in Majorca Alfonso watched the door.

GERARD MANLEY HOPKINS

On the Death of Dr Robert Levet

Condemn'd to hope's delusive mine,
   As on we toil from day to day,
By sudden blasts, or slow decline,
   Our social comforts drop away.

Well tried through many a varying year,
   See LEVET to the grave descend;
Officious, innocent, sincere,
   Of ev'ry friendless name the friend.

Yet still he fills affection's eye,
   Obscurely wise, and coarsely kind;
Nor, letter'd arrogance, deny
   Thy praise to merit unrefin'd.

When fainting nature call'd for aid,
   And hov'ring death prepar'd the blow,
His vig'rous remedy display'd
   The power of art without the show.

In misery's darkest caverns known,
   His useful care was ever nigh,
Where hopeless anguish pour'd his groan,
   And lonely want retir'd to die.

No summons mock'd by chill delay,
   No petty gain disdain'd by pride,
The modest wants of ev'ry day
   The toil of ev'ry day supplied.

His virtues walk'd their narrow round,
   Nor made a pause, nor left a void;
And sure th'Eternal Master found
   The single talent well employed.

The busy day, the peaceful night,
  Unfelt, uncounted, glided by;
His frame was firm, his powers were bright,
  Tho' now his eightieth year was nigh.

Then with no throbbing fiery pain,
  No cold gradations of decay,
Death broke at once the vital chain,
  And free'd his soul the nearest way.

SAMUEL JOHNSON

Hamlet (Act V, sc i)

LAERTES: What ceremony else?
PRIEST: Her obsequies have been as far enlarg'd
As we have warrantise. Her death was doubtful;
And, but that great command o'ersways the order,
She should in ground unsanctified have lodg'd
Till the last trumpet; for charitable prayers,
Shards, flints, and pebbles, should be thrown on her;
Yet here she is allow'd her virgin crants,
Her maiden strewments, and the bringing home
Of bell and burial.
LAERTES: Must there no more be done?
PRIEST: No more be done.
We should profane the service of the dead
To sing sage requiem and such rest to her
As to peace-parted souls.
LAERTES: Lay her i' th' earth;
And from her fair and unpolluted flesh
May violets spring! I tell thee, churlish priest,
A minist'ring angel shall my sister be
When thou liest howling.

WILLIAM SHAKESPEARE

On the University Carrier

On the University Carrier who sickn'd in the time of
his vacancy, being forbid to go to *London*, by reason
of the Plague.

Here lies old *Hobson*, Death hath broke his girt,
And here alas, hath laid him in the dirt,
Or els the ways being foul, twenty to one,
He's here stuck in a slough, and overthrown.
'Twas such a shifter, that if truth were known,
Death was half glad when he had got him down;
For he had any time this ten yeers full,
Dodg'd with him, betwixt *Cambridge* and the Bull.
And surely, Death could never have prevail'd,
Had not his weekly cours of carriage fail'd;
But lately finding him so long at home,
And thinking now his journeys end was come,
And that he had tane up his latest Inne,
In the kind office of a Chamberlin
Shew'd him his room where he must lodge that night,
Pull'd off his Boots, and took away the light:
If any ask for him, it shall be sed,
Hobson has supt, and's newly gon to bed.

JOHN MILTON

PRINCE: Dost thou speak like a king? Do thou stand for
          me, and I'll play my father.

FALSTAFF: Depose me? If thou dost it half so gravely, so
          majestically, both in word and matter, hang
          me up by the heels for a rabbit-sucker or a
          poulter's hare.

PRINCE: Well, here I am set.

FALSTAFF: And here I stand. Judge, my masters.

PRINCE: Now, Harry, whence come you?

FALSTAFF: My noble lord, from Eastcheap.

PRINCE: The complaints I hear of thee are grievous.

FALSTAFF: 'Sblood, my lord, they are false. Nay, I'll tickle
          ye for a young prince, i' faith.

PRINCE: Swearest thou, ungracious boy? Henceforth
          ne'er look on me. Thou art violently carried
          away from grace; there is a devil haunts thee
          in the likeness of an old fat man; a tun of man
          is thy companion. Why dost thou converse
          with that trunk of humours, that bolting-hutch
          of beastliness, that swoll'n parcel of dropsies,
          that huge bombard of sack, that stuff'd cloak-
          bag of guts, that roasted Manningtree ox with
          the pudding in his belly, that reverend vice,
          that grey iniquity, that father ruffian, that
          vanity in years? Wherein is he good, but to
          taste sack and drink it? wherein neat and
          cleanly, but to carve a capon and eat it?
          wherein cunning, but in craft? wherein crafty,
          but in villainy? wherein villainous, but in all
          things? wherein worthy, but in nothing?

FALSTAFF: I would your Grace would take me with you;
          whom means your Grace?

PRINCE: That villainous abominable misleader of youth,
          Falstaff, that old whitebearded Satan.

FALSTAFF: My lord, the man I know.

PRINCE: I know thou dost.

FALSTAFF: But to say I know more harm in him than in myself were to say more than I know. That he is old—the more the pity—his white hairs do witness it; but that he is—saving your reverence—a whoremaster, that I utterly deny. If sack and sugar be a fault, God help the wicked! If to be old and merry be a sin, then many an old host that I know is damn'd; if to be fat be to be hated, then Pharaoh's lean kine are to be loved. No, my good lord: banish Peto, banish Bardolph, banish Poins; but, for sweet Jack Falstaff, kind Jack Falstaff, true Jack Falstaff, valiant Jack Falstaff—and therefore more valiant, being, as he is, old Jack Falstaff— banish not him thy Harry's company, banish not him thy Harry's company. Banish plump Jack, and banish all the world.

PRINCE: I do, I will.

WILLIAM SHAKESPEARE

Henry V (Act II, sc iii)

PISTOL:	Boy, bristle thy courage up. For Falstaff he is dead, And we must earn therefore.
BARDOLPH:	Would I were with him, wheresome'er he is, either in heaven or in hell!
HOSTESS:	Nay, sure, he's not in hell: he's in Arthur's bosom, if ever man went to Arthur's bosom. 'A made a finer end, and went away an it had been any christom child; 'a parted ev'n just between twelve and one, ev'n at the turning o' th' tide; for after I saw him fumble with the sheets, and play with flowers, and smile upon his fingers' end, I knew there was but one way; for his nose was as sharp as a pen, and 'a babbl'd of green fields. 'How now, Sir John!' quoth I, 'What, man, be o' good cheer.' So 'a cried out 'God, God, God!' three or four times. Now I, to comfort him, bid him 'a should not think of God; I hop'd there was no need to trouble himself with any such thoughts yet. So 'a bade me lay more clothes on his feet; I put my hand into the bed and felt them, and they were as cold as any stone; then I felt to his knees, and so upward and upward, and all was as cold as any stone.
NYM:	They say he cried out of sack.
HOSTESS:	Ay, that 'a did.
BARDOLPH:	And of women.
HOSTESS:	Nay, that 'a did not.
BOY:	Yes, that 'a did, and said they were devils incarnate.
HOSTESS:	'A could never abide carnation; 'twas a colour he never lik'd.
BOY:	'A said once the devil would have him about women.

HOSTESS:	'A did in some sort, indeed, handle women; but then he was rheumatic, and talk'd of the Whore of Babylon.
BOY:	Do you not remember 'a saw a flea stick upon Bardolph's nose, and 'a said it was a black soul burning in hell?
BARDOLPH:	Well, the fuel is gone that maintain'd that fire: that's all the riches I got in his service.

WILLIAM SHAKESPEARE

Othello (Act V, sc ii)

OTHELLO: Soft you; a word or two before you go.
I have done the state some service, and they know't—
No more of that. I pray you, in your letters,
When you shall these unlucky deeds relate,
Speak of me as I am; nothing extenuate,
Nor set down aught in malice. Then must you speak
Of one that lov'd not wisely, but too well;
Of one not easily jealous, but, being wrought,
Perplexed in the extreme; of one whose hand,
Like the base Indian, threw a pearl away
Richer than all his tribe; of one whose subdu'd eyes,
Albeit unused to the melting mood,
Drops tears as fast as the Arabian trees
Their med'cinable gum. Set you down this:
And say besides that in Aleppo once,
Where a malignant and a turban'd Turk
Beat a Venetian and traduc'd the state,
I took by th' throat the circumcised dog,
And smote him—thus.   [*He stabs himself.*

WILLIAM SHAKESPEARE

Sonnet LXXI

No longer mourn for me when I am dead
Than you shall hear the surly sullen bell
Give warning to the world that I am fled
From this vile world, with vilest worms to dwell:
Nay, if you read this line, remember not
The hand that writ it; for I love you so,
That I in your sweet thoughts would be forgot,
If thinking on me then should make you woe.
O! if,—I say, you look upon this verse,
When I perhaps compounded am with clay,
Do not so much as my poor name rehearse,
But let your love even with my life decay;
  Lest the wise world should look into your moan,
  And mock you with me after I am gone.

WILLIAM SHAKESPEARE

Come Not, When I am Dead

Come not, when I am dead,
  To drop thy foolish tears upon my grave,
To trample round my fallen head,
  And vex the unhappy dust thou wouldst not save.
There let the wind sweep and the plover cry;
    But thou, go by.

Child, if it were thine error or thy crime
  I care no longer, being all unblest:
Wed whom thou wilt, but I am sick of Time,
  And I desire to rest.
Pass on, weak heart, and leave me where I lie:
    Go by, go by.

ALFRED, LORD TENNYSON

At the Round Earth's Imagined Corners

At the round earth's imagined corners, blow
Your trumpets, angels, and arise, arise
From death, you numberless infinities
Of souls, and to your scattered bodies go,
All whom the flood did, and fire shall o'erthrow,
All whom war, dearth, age, agues, tyrannies,
Despair, law, chance, hath slain, and you whose eyes,
Shall behold God, and never taste death's woe.

But let them sleep, Lord, and me mourn a space,
For, if above all these, my sins abound,
'Tis late to ask abundance of thy grace,
When we are there; here on this lowly ground,
Teach me how to repent; for that's as good
As if thou hadst sealed my pardon, with thy blood.

JOHN DONNE

Jimmy's Enlisted
or
The Recruited Collier

Oh, what's the matter wi' you, my lass,
    An' where's your dashin Jimmy?
The sowdger boys have picked him up
    And sent him far, far frae me.

Last pay-day he set off to town,
    And them red-coated fellows
Enticed him in and made him drunk,
    And he'd better gone to the gallows.

The very sight o' his cockade,
  It set us all a-cryin;
And me, I fairly fainted twice,
  I thought that I was dyin.

My father would have paid the smart,
  And run for the golden guinea,
But the sergeant swore he'd kissed the book,
  And now they've got young Jimmy.

When Jimmy talks about the wars
  It's worse than death to hear him.
I must go out and hide my tears,
  Because I cannot bear him.

For aye he jibes and cracks his jokes,
  And bids me not forsake him.
A brigadier or grenadier,
  He says they're sure to make him.

As I walked over the stubble field,
  Below it runs the seam,
I thought o' Jimmy hewin there,
  But it was all a dream.

He hewed the very coals we burn,
  And when the fire I'se leetin,
To think the lumps was in his hands,
  It sets my heart to beatin.

So break my heart, and then it's ower,
  So break my heart, my dearie,
And I'll lie in the cold, cold grave,
  For of single life I'm weary.

ANON

The Explosion

On the day of the explosion
Shadows pointed towards the pithead:
In the sun the slagheap slept.

Down the lane came men in pitboots
Coughing oath-edged talk and pipe-smoke,
Shouldering off the freshened silence.

One chased after rabbits; lost them;
Came back with a nest of lark's eggs;
Showed them; lodged them in the grasses.

So they passed in beards and moleskins,
Fathers, brothers, nicknames, laughter,
Through the tall gates standing open.

At noon, there came a tremor; cows
Stopped chewing for a second; sun,
Scarfed as in a heat-haze, dimmed.

The dead go on before us, they
Are sitting in God's house in comfort,
We shall see them face to face—

Plain as lettering in the chapels
It was said, and for a second
Wives saw men of the explosion

Larger than in life they managed—
Gold as on a coin, or walking
Somehow from the sun towards them,

One showing the eggs unbroken.

PHILIP LARKIN

Felix Randal

Felix Randal the farrier, O he is dead then? my duty all
    ended,
Who have watched his mould of man, big-boned and
    hardy-handsome
Pining, pining, till time when reason rambled in it and some
Fatal four disorders, fleshed there, all contended?

Sickness broke him. Impatient he cursed at first, but mended
Being anointed and all; though a heavenlier heart began
    some
Months earlier, since I had our sweet reprieve and ransom
Tendered to him. Ah well, God rest him all road ever he
    offended!

This seeing the sick endears them to us, us too it endears.
My tongue had taught thee comfort, touch had quenched
    thy tears,
Thy tears that touched my heart, child, Felix, poor Felix
    Randal;
How far from then forethought of, all thy more boisterous
    years,
When thou at the random grim forge, powerful amidst
    peers,   .
Didst fettle for the great grey drayhorse his bright and
    battering sandal!

GERARD MANLEY HOPKINS

Northern Farmer
New Style

I

Dosn't thou 'ear my 'erse's legs, as they canters awaäy?
Proputty, proputty, proputty–that's what I 'ears 'em saäy.
Proputty, proputty, proputty–Sam, thou's an ass for thy
    paaïns:
Theer's moor sense i' one o' 'is legs nor in all thy braaïns.

II

Woä–theer's a craw to pluck wi' tha, Sam: yon's parson's
    'ouse–
Dosn't thou knaw that a man mun be eäther a man or a
    mouse?
Time to think on it then; for thou'll be twenty to weeäk.
Proputty, proputty–woä then woä–let ma 'ear mysén
    speäk.

III

Me an' thy muther, Sammy, 'as beän a-talkin' o' thee;
Thou's beän talkin' to muther, an' she beän a tellin' it me.
Thou'll not marry for munny–thou's sweet upo' parson's
    lass–
Noä–thou'll marry for luvv–an' we boäth on us thinks tha
    an ass.

IV

Seeä'd her todaäy goä by–Saäint's-daäy–they was ringing
    the bells.
She's a beauty thou thinks–an' soä is scoors o' gells,
Them as 'as munny an' all–wot's a beauty?–the flower as
    blaws.
But proputty, proputty sticks, an' proputty, proputty graws.

Do'ant be stunt: taäke time: I knaws what maäkes tha sa
   mad.
Warn't I craäzed fur the lasses mysén when I wur a lad?
But I knawed a Quaäker feller as often 'as towd ma this:
'Doänt thou marry for munny, but goä wheer munny is!'

An' I went wheer munny war: an' thy muther coom to 'and,
Wi' lots o' munny laaïd by, an' a nicetish bit o' land.
Maäybe she warn't a beauty:–I niver giv it a thowt–
But warn't she as good to cuddle an' kiss as a lass as 'ant
   nowt?

Parson's lass 'ant nowt, an' she weänt 'a nowt when 'e's
   deäd,
Mun be a guvness, lad, or summut, and addle her breäd:
Why? fur 'e's nobbut a curate, an' weänt niver git hissen
   clear,
An' 'e maäde the bed as 'e ligs on afoor 'e coomed to the
   shere.

An' thin 'e coomed to the parish wi' lots o' Varsity debt,
Stook to his taaïl they did, an' 'e 'ant go shut on 'em yet,
An' 'e ligs on 'is back i' the grip, wi' noän to lend 'im a
   shuvv,
Woorse nor a far-weltered yowe: fur, Sammy, 'e married
   fur luvv.

Luvv? what's luvv? thou can luvv thy lass an' 'er munny
   too,
Maakin' 'em goä togither as they've good right to do.
Could'n I luvv thy muther by cause o' 'er munny laaïd by?
Naäy–fur I luvved 'er a vast sight moor fur it: reäson why.

X

Ay an' thy muther says thou wants to marry the lass,
Cooms of a gentleman burn: an' we boäth on us think tha
    an ass.
Woä then, proputty, wiltha?–an ass as near as mays nowt–
Woä then, wiltha? dangtha!–the bees is as fell as owt.

XI

Breäk me a bit o' the esh for his 'eäd lad, out o' the fence!
Gentleman burn! what's gentleman burn? is it shillins an'
    pence?
Proputty, proputty's ivrything 'ere, an', Sammy, I'm blest
If it isn't the saäme oop yonder, fur them as 'as it's the best.

XII

Tis'n them as 'as munny as breäks into 'ouses an' steäls,
Them as 'as coäts to their backs an' taäkes their regular
    meäls.
Noä, but it's them as niver knaws wheer a meäl's to be 'ad.
Taäke my word for it, Sammy, the poor in a loomp is bad.

XIII

Them or thir feythers, tha sees, mun 'a beän a laäzy lot,
Fur work mun 'a gone to the gittin' whiniver munny was
    got.
Feyther 'ad ammost nowt; leästways 'is munny was 'id.
But 'e tued an' moiled 'issén deäd, an 'e died a good un,
    'e did.

XIV

Look thou theer wheer Wrigglesby beck cooms out by the
    'ill!
Feyther run oop to the farm, an' I runs oop to the mill;
An' I'll run oop to the brig, an' that thou'll live to see;
And if thou marries a good un I'll leäve the land to thee.

XV

Thim's my noätions, Sammy, wheerby I means to stick;
But if thou marries a bad un, I'll leäve the land to Dick.-
Coom oop, proputty, proputty–that's what I 'ears 'im
    saäy–
Proputty, proputty, proputty–canter an' canter awaäy.

ALFRED, LORD TENNYSON

Henry VI, Part III (Act II, sc v)

KING HENRY: O God! methinks it were a happy life
To be no better than a homely swain;
To sit upon a hill, as I do now,
To carve out dials quaintly, point by point,
Thereby to see the minutes how they run—
How many makes the hour full complete,
How many hours brings about the day,
How many days will finish up the year,
How many years a mortal man may live.
When this is known, then to divide the times—
So many hours must I tend my flock;
So many hours must I take my rest;
So many hours must I contemplate;
So many hours must I sport myself;
So many days my ewes have been with young;
So many weeks ere the poor fools will ean;
So many years ere I shall shear the fleece:
So minutes, hours, days, months, and years,
Pass'd over to the end they were created,
Would bring white hairs unto a quiet grave.
Ah, what a life were this! how sweet! how lovely!
Gives not the hawthorn bush a sweeter shade
To shepherds looking on their silly sheep,
Than doth a rich embroider'd canopy
To kings that fear their subjects' treachery?

WILLIAM SHAKESPEARE

With Seed the Sowers Scatter

(XXXII)

With seed the sowers scatter
 The furrows as they go;
Poor lads, 'tis little matter
 How many sorts they sow,
 For only one will grow.

The charlock on the fallow
 Will take the traveller's eyes,
And gild the ploughland sallow
 With flowers before it dies,
 But twice 'twill not arise.

The stinging nettle only
 Will still be found to stand:
The numberless, the lonely,
 The thronger of the land,
 The leaf that hurts the hand.

That thrives, come sun, come showers;
 Blow east, blow west, it springs;
It peoples towns, and towers
 About the courts of Kings,
 And touch it and it stings.

A. E. HOUSMAN

The Mower against Gardens

Luxurious Man, to bring his Vice in use,
 Did after him the World seduce:
And from the fields the Flow'rs and Plants allure,
 Where Nature was most plain and pure.
He first enclos'd within the Gardens square
 A dead and standing pool of Air:
And a more luscious Earth for them did knead,
 Which stupifi'd them while it fed.
The Pink grew then as double as his Mind;

The nutriment did change the kind.
With strange perfumes he did the Roses taint.
  And Flow'rs themselves were taught to paint.
The Tulip, white, did for complexion seek;
  And learn'd to interline its cheek:
Its Onion root they then so high did hold,
  That one was for a Meadow sold.
Another World was search'd, through Oceans new,
  To find the *Marvel of Peru*.
And yet these Rarities might be allow'd,
  To Man, that sov'raign thing and proud;
Had he not dealt between the Bark and Tree,
  Forbidden mixtures there to see.
No Plant now knew the Stock from which it came;
  He grafts upon the Wild the Tame:
That the uncertain and adult'rate fruit
  Might put the Palate in dispute.
His green *Seraglio* has its Eunuchs too;
  Lest any Tyrant him out-doe.
And in the Cherry he does Nature vex,
  To procreate without a Sex.
'Tis all enforc'd; the Fountain and the Grot;
  While the sweet Fields do lye forgot:
Where willing Nature does to all dispence
  A wild and fragrant Innocence:
And *Fauns* and *Faryes* do the Meadows till,
  More by their presence then their skill.
Their Statues polish'd by some ancient hand,
  May to adorn the Gardens stand:
But howso'ere the Figures do excel,
  The *Gods* themselves with us do dwell.

ANDREW MARVELL

The Tempest (Act V, sc i)

PROSPERO: Ye elves of hills, brooks, standing lakes, and
            groves;
And ye that on the sands with printless foot
Do chase the ebbing Neptune, and do fly him
When he comes back; you demi-puppets that
By moonshine do the green sour ringlets make,
Whereof the ewe not bites; and you whose pastime
Is to make midnight mushrooms, that rejoice
To hear the solemn curfew; by whose aid—
Weak masters though ye be—I have bedimm'd
The noontide sun, call'd forth the mutinous winds,
And 'twixt the green sea and the azur'd vault
Set roaring war. To the dread rattling thunder
Have I given fire, and rifted Jove's stout oak
With his own bolt; the strong-bas'd promontory
Have I made shake, and by the spurs pluck'd up
The pine and cedar. Graves at my command
Have wak'd their sleepers, op'd, and let 'em forth,
By my so potent art. But this rough magic
I here abjure; and, when I have requir'd
Some heavenly music—which even now I do—
To work mine end upon their senses that
This airy charm is for, I'll break my staff,
Bury it certain fathoms in the earth,
And deeper than did ever plummet sound
I'll drown my book.

WILLIAM SHAKESPEARE

From Paradise Lost (Book III)

Mean while upon the firm opacous Globe
Of this round World, whose first convex divides
The luminous inferior Orbs, enclos'd
From *Chaos* and th' inroad of Darkness old,
Satan alighted walks: a Globe farr off
It seem'd, now seems a boundless Continent
Dark, waste, and wild, under the frown of Night
Starless expos'd, and ever-threatning storms
Of *Chaos* blustring round, inclement skie;
Save on that side which from the wall of Heav'n
Though distant farr som small reflection gaines
Of glimmering air less vext with tempest loud:
Here walk'd the Fiend at large in spacious field.
As when a Vultur on *Imaus* bred,
Whose snowie ridge the roving *Tartar* bounds,
Dislodging from a Region scarce of prey
To gorge the flesh of Lambs or yeanling Kids
On Hills where Flocks are fed, flies toward the Springs
Of *Ganges* or *Hydaspes*, *Indian* streams;
But in his way lights on the barren plaines
Of *Sericana*, where *Chineses* drive
With Sails and Wind thir canie Waggons light:
So on this windie Sea of Land, the Fiend
Walk'd up and down alone bent on his prey,
Alone, for other Creature in this place
Living or liveless to be found was none,
None yet, but store hereafter from the earth
Up hither like Aereal vapours flew
Of all things transitorie and vain, when Sin
With vanity had filld the works of men:
Both all things vain, and all who in vain things
Built thir fond hopes of Glorie or lasting fame,
Or happiness in this or th' other life;
All who have thir reward on Earth, the fruits
Of painful Superstition and blind Zeal,

Naught seeking but the praise of men, here find
Fit retribution, emptie as thir deeds;
All th' unaccomplisht works of Natures hand,
Abortive, monstrous, or unkindly mixt,
Dissolvd on earth, fleet hither, and in vain,
Till final dissolution, wander here,
Not in the neighbouring Moon, as some have dreamd;
Those argent Fields more likely habitants,
Translated Saints, or middle Spirits hold
Betwixt th' Angelical and Human kinde:
Hither of ill-joynd Sons and Daughters born
First from the ancient World those Giants came
With many a vain exploit, though then renownd:
The builders next of *Babel* on the Plain
Of *Sennaar*, and still with vain designe
New *Babels*, had they wherewithall, would build:
Others came single; hee who to be deemd
A God, leap'd fondly into *Ætna* flames
Empedocles, and hee who to enjoy
Plato's Elysium, leap'd into the Sea,
Cleombrotus, and many more too long,
Embryo's, and Idiots, Eremits and Friers
White, Black and Grey, with all thir trumperie.
Here Pilgrims roam, that stray'd so farr to seek
In *Golgotha* him dead, who lives in Heav'n;
And they who to be sure of Paradise
Dying put on the weeds of *Dominic*,
Or in *Franciscan* think to pass disguis'd;
They pass the Planets seven, and pass the fixt,
And that Crystalline Sphear whose ballance weighs
The Trepidation talkt, and that first mov'd;
And now Saint *Peter* at Heav'ns Wicket seems
To wait them with his Keys, and now at foot
Of Heav'ns ascent they lift thir Feet, when loe
A violent cross wind from either Coast
Blows them transverse ten thousand Leagues awry
Into the devious Air; then might ye see
Cowles, Hoods and Habits with thir wearers tost

And fluttered into Raggs, then Reliques, Beads,
Indulgences, Dispenses, Pardons, Bulls,
The sport of Winds: all these upwhirld aloft
Fly o're the backside of the World farr off
Into a *Limbo* large and broad, since calld
The Paradise of Fools, to few unknown
Long after, now unpeopl'd, and untrod;
All this dark Globe the Fiend found as he pass'd,
And long he wanderd, till at last a gleame
Of dawning light turnd thither-ward in haste
His travell'd steps; farr distant hee descries
Ascending by degrees magnificent
Up to the wall of Heaven a Structure high,
At top whereof, but farr more rich appeerd
The work as of a Kingly Palace Gate
With Frontispice of Diamond and Gold
Imbellisht, thick with sparkling orient Gemmes
The Portal shon, inimitable on Earth
By Model, or by shading Pencil drawn.
The Stairs were such as whereon *Jacob* saw
Angels ascending and descending, bands
Of Guardians bright, when he from *Esau* fled
To *Padan-Aram* in the field of *Luz*,
Dreaming by night under the open Skie,
And waking cri'd, This is the Gate of Heav'n.

JOHN MILTON

Sumer is icumen in

    Sing! cuccu, nu. Sing! cuccu.
    Sing! cuccu. Sing! cuccu, nu.

Sumer is icumen in—
Lhude sing! cuccu.
Groweth sed and bloweth med
And springth the wude nu—
Sing! cuccu.

Awe bleteth after lomb,
Lhouth after calve cu,
Bulluc sterteth, bucke verteth,
Murie sing! cuccu.
Cuccu, cuccu,
Well singes thu, cuccu—
Ne swik thu naver nu!

ANON (early 13th century)

Ancient Music

Winter is icummen in,
Lhude sing Goddamm,
Raineth drop and staineth slop,
And how the wind doth ramm!
        Sing: Goddamm.
Skiddeth bus and sloppeth us,
An ague hath my ham.
Freezeth river, turneth liver,
        Damn you, sing: Goddamm.
Goddamm, Goddamm, 'tis why I am, Goddamm.
        So 'gainst the winter's balm.
Sing goddamm, damm, sing Goddamm,
Sing goddamm, sing goddamm, DAMM.

EZRA POUND

From Winter

Wind piercing, hill bare, hard to find shelter;
    Ford turns foul, lake freezes.
A man could stand on a stalk.

    Wave on wave cloaks the land's edge;
Shrill the shrieks from the peaks of the mountain;
    One can scarce stand outside.

201

Cold the lake-bed from winter's blast;
    Dried reeds, stalks broken;
    Angry wind, woods stripped naked.

Cold bed of fish beneath a screen of ice;
    Stag lean, stalks bearded;
    Short evening, trees bent over.

        Snow is falling, white the soil.
        Soldiers go not campaigning.
        Cold lakes, their colour sunless.

        Snow is falling, white hoar-frost.
        Shield idle on an old shoulder.
        Wind intense, shoots are frozen.

        Snow is falling upon the ice.
        Wind is sweeping thick tree-tops.
        Shield bold on a brave shoulder.

        Snow is falling, cloaks the valley.
        Soldiers hasten to battle.
        I go not, a wound stays me.

        Snow is falling on the slope.
        Stallion confined; lean cattle.
        No summer day is today.

Snow is falling, white the mountain's edge.
    Ship's mast bare at sea.
    A coward conceives many schemes.

                    ANON
                    FROM A 13TH CENTURY MS
                    TRANSLATED FROM THE WELSH
                    BY JOSEPH CLANCY

Cold Weather Proverb

Fearless approach and puffed feather
In birds, famine bespeak;
In man, belly filled full.

ROBERT GRAVES

Swedes

They have taken the gable from the roof of clay
On the long swede pile. They have let in the sun
To the white and gold and purple of curled fronds
Unsunned. It is a sight more tender-gorgeous
At the wood-corner where Winter moans and drips
Than when, in the Valley of the Tombs of Kings,
A boy crawls down into a Pharaoh's tomb
And, first of Christian men, beholds the mummy,
God and monkey, chariot and throne and vase,
Blue pottery, alabaster, and gold.

But dreamless long-dead Amen-hotep lies.
This is a dream of Winter, sweet as Spring.

EDWARD THOMAS

Fish in the Unruffled Lakes

Fish in the unruffled lakes
The swarming colours wear,
Swans in the winter air
A white perfection have,
And the great lion walks
Through his innocent grove;
Lion, fish, and swan
Act, and are gone
Upon Time's toppling wave.

We till shadowed days are done,
We must weep and sing
Duty's conscious wrong,
The Devil in the clock,
The Goodness carefully worn
For atonement or for luck;
We must lose our loves,
On each beast and bird that moves
Turn an envious look.

Sighs for folly said and done
Twist our narrow days;
But I must bless, I must praise
That you, my swan, who have
All gifts that to the swan
Impulsive Nature gave,
The majesty and pride,
Last night should add
Your voluntary love.

W. H. AUDEN

Thaw

Over the land freckled with snow half-thawed
The speculating rooks at their nests cawed
And saw from elm-tops, delicate as flower of grass,
What we below could not see, Winter pass.

EDWARD THOMAS

Binsey Poplars

Felled 1879

My aspens dear, whose airy cages quelled,
Quelled or quenched in leaves the leaping sun,
All felled, felled, are all felled;
   Of a fresh and following folded rank
      Not spared, not one
      That dandled a sandalled
    Shadow that swam or sank
On meadow and river and wind-wandering weed-winding
   bank.

O if we but knew what we do
    When we delve or hew—
   Hack and rack the growing green!
     Since country is so tender
  To touch, her being só slender,
  That, like this sleek and seeing ball
  But a prick will make no eye at all,
  Where we, even where we mean
     To mend her we end her,
   When we hew or delve:
After-comers cannot guess the beauty been.
  Ten or twelve, only ten or twelve
   Strokes of havoc unselve
    The sweet especial scene,
   Rural scene, a rural scene,
   Sweet especial rural scene.

GERARD MANLEY HOPKINS

In Rivum a Mola Stoana Lichfeldiæ diffluentem

Errat adhuc vitreus per prata virentia rivus,
　　Quo toties lavi membra tenella puer;
Hic delusa rudi frustrabar brachia motu,
　　Dum docuit blanda voce natare pater.
Fecerunt rami latebras, tenebrisque diurnis
　　Pendula secretas abdidit arbor aquas.
Nunc veteres duris periere securibus umbræ,
　　Longinquisque oculis nuda lavacra patent,
Lympha tamen cursus agit indefessa perennis,
　　Tectaque qua fluxit, nunc et aperta fluit.
Quid ferat externi velox, quid deterat ætas,
　　Tu quoque securus res age, Nise, tuas.

SAMUEL JOHNSON

By the River, at Stowe Mill, Lichfield, Where the Streams Flow Together

Clear as glass the stream still wanders through
green fields.
　　　　　Here, as a boy, I bathed
my tender limbs, unskilled, frustrated, while
with gentle voice my father from the bank
taught me to swim.
　　　　　The branches made
a hiding-place: the bending trees concealed
the water in a daytime darkness.
　　　　　　　　Now
hard axes have destroyed those ancient shades:
the pool lies naked, even to distant eyes.

But the water, never tiring, still runs on
in the same channel: once hidden, now overt,
always flowing.
                    Nisus, you too, what time
brings from outside, or wears away within
ignoring, do the things you have to do.

TRANS. J. W.

The Self-Unseeing

Here is the ancient floor,
Footworn and hollowed and thin,
Here was the former door
Where the dead feet walked in.

She sat here in her chair,
Smiling into the fire;
He who played stood there,
Bowing it higher and higher.

Childlike, I danced in a dream;
Blessings emblazoned that day;
Everything glowed with a gleam;
Yet we were looking away!

THOMAS HARDY

Into My Heart

Into my heart an air that kills
From yon far country blows:
What are those blue remembered hills,
What spires, what farms are those?

That is the land of lost content,
I see it shining plain,
The happy highways where I went
And cannot come again.

A. E. HOUSMAN

Richard II (Act I, sc iii)

KING RICHARD: Norfolk, for thee remains a heavier doom,
Which I with some unwillingness pronounce:
The sly slow hours shall not determinate
The dateless limit of thy dear exile;
The hopeless word of 'never to return'
Breathe I against thee, upon pain of life.
MOWBRAY: A heavy sentence, my most sovereign liege,
And all unlook'd for from your Highness' mouth.
A dearer merit, not so deep a maim
As to be cast forth in the common air,
Have I deserved at your Highness' hands.
The language I have learnt these forty years,
My native English, now I must forgo;

And now my tongue's use is to me no more
Than an unstringed viol or a harp;
Or like a cunning instrument cas'd up
Or, being open, put into his hands
That knows no touch to tune the harmony.
Within my mouth you have engaol'd my tongue,
Doubly portcullis'd with my teeth and lips;
And dull, unfeeling, barren ignorance
Is made my gaoler to attend on me.
I am too old to fawn upon a nurse,
Too far in years to be a pupil now.
What is thy sentence, then, but speechless death,
Which robs my tongue from breathing native breath?

WILLIAM SHAKESPEARE

The Candle Indoors

Some candle clear burns somewhere I come by.
I muse at how its being puts blissful back
With yellowy moisture mild night's blear-all black,
Or to-fro tender trambeams truckle at the eye.
By that window what task what fingers ply,
I plod wondering, a-wanting, just for lack
Of answer the eagerer a-wanting Jessy or Jack
There   God to aggrándise, God to glorify.—

Come you indoors, come home; your fading fire
Mend first and vital candle in close heart's vault:
You there are master, do your own desire;
What hinders? Are you beam-blind, yet to a fault
In a neighbour deft-handed? are you that liar
And, cast by conscience out, spendsavour salt?

GERARD MANLEY HOPKINS

209

Now Winter Nights

Now winter nights enlarge
  The number of their houres,
And clouds their stormes discharge
  Upon the ayrie towres;
Let now the chimneys blaze
  And cups o'erflow with wine,
Let well-tun'd words amaze
  With harmonie divine.
Now yellow waxen lights
  Shall waite on hunny Love,
While youthfull Revels, Masks, and Courtly sights,
  Sleepes leaden spels remove.

This time doth well dispence
  With lovers long discourse;
Much speech hath some defence,
  Though beauty no remorse.
All doe not all things well:
  Some measures comely tread,
Some knotted Ridles tell,
  Some Poems smoothly read.
The Summer hath his joyes,
  And Winter his delights;
Though Love and all his pleasures are but toyes,
  They shorten tedious nights.

THOMAS CAMPION

Lawrence of Vertuous Father

Lawrence of vertuous Father vertuous Son,
  Now that the Fields are dank, and ways are mire,
  Where shall we sometimes meet, and by the fire
  Help wast a sullen day; what may be won
From the hard Season gaining: time will run
  On smoother, till *Favonius* re-inspire
  The frozen earth; and cloth in fresh attire
  The Lillie and Rose, that neither sow'd nor spun.
What neat repast shall feast us, light and choice,
  Of Attick tast, with Wine, whence we may rise
  To hear the Lute well toucht, or artfull voice
Warble immortal Notes and *Tuskan* Ayre?
  He who of those delights can judge, and spare
  To interpose them oft, is not unwise.

JOHN MILTON

All Souls' Night

Epilogue to A Vision

Midnight has come, and the great Christ Church Bell
And many a lesser bell sound through the room;
And it is All Souls' Night,
And two long glasses brimmed with muscatel
Bubble upon the table. A ghost may come;
For it is a ghost's right,
His element is so fine
Being sharpened by his death,
To drink from the wine-breath
While our gross palates drink from the whole wine.
I need some mind that, if the cannon sound
From every quarter of the world, can stay
Wound in mind's pondering
As mummies in the mummy-cloth are wound;

Because I have a marvellous thing to say,
A certain marvellous thing
None but the living mock,
Though not for sober ear;
It may be all that hear
Should laugh and weep an hour upon the clock.

Horton's the first I call. He loved strange thought
And knew that sweet extremity of pride
That's called platonic love,
And that to such a pitch of passion wrought
Nothing could bring him, when his lady died,
Anodyne for his love.
Words were but wasted breath;
One dear hope had he:
The inclemency
Of that or the next winter would be death.

Two thoughts were so mixed up I could not tell
Whether of her or God he thought the most,
But think that his mind's eye,
When upward turned, on one sole image fell;
And that a slight companionable ghost,
Wild with divinity,
Had so lit up the whole
Immense miraculous house
The Bible promised us,
It seemed a gold-fish swimming in a bowl.

On Florence Emery I call the next,
Who finding the first wrinkles on a face
Admired and beautiful,
And knowing that the future would be vexed
With 'minished beauty, multiplied commonplace,
Preferred to teach a school
Away from neighbour or friend,
Among dark skins, and there
Permit foul years to wear
Hidden from eyesight to the unnoticed end.

Before that end much had she ravelled out
From a discourse in figurative speech
By some learned Indian
On the soul's journey. How it is whirled about,
Wherever the orbit of the moon can reach,
Until it plunge into the sun;
And there, free and yet fast,
Being both Chance and Choice,
Forget its broken toys
And sink into its own delight at last.

And I call up MacGregor from the grave,
For in my first hard springtime we were friends,
Although of late estranged.
I thought him half a lunatic, half knave,
And told him so, but friendship never ends;
And what if mind seem changed,
And it seem changed with the mind,
When thoughts rise up unbid
On generous things that he did
And I grow half contented to be blind!

He had much industry at setting out,
Much boisterous courage, before loneliness
Had driven him crazed;
For meditations upon unknown thought
Make human intercourse grow less and less;
They are neither paid nor praised.
But he'd object to the host,
The glass because my glass;
A ghost-lover he was
And may have grown more arrogant being a ghost.

But names are nothing. What matter who it be,
So that his elements have grown so fine
The fume of muscatel
Can give his sharpened palate ecstasy.
No living man can drink from the whole wine.
I have mummy truths to tell
Whereat the living mock,
Though not for sober ear,
For maybe all that hear
Should laugh and weep an hour upon the clock.

Such thought—such thought have I that hold it tight
Till meditation master all its parts,
Nothing can stay my glance
Until that glance run in the world's despite
To where the damned have howled away their hearts,
And where the blessed dance;
Such thought, that in it bound
I need no other thing,
Wound in mind's wandering
As mummies in the mummy-cloth are wound.

W. B. YEATS

Duns Scotus's Oxford

Towery city and branchy between towers;
Cuckoo-echoing, bell-swarmèd, lark-charmèd, rook-racked,
    river-rounded;
The dapple-eared lily below thee; that country and town
    did
Once encounter in, here coped and poisèd powers;

Thou hast a base and brickish skirt there, sours
That neighbour-nature thy grey beauty is grounded
Best in; graceless growth, thou hast confounded
Rural rural keeping—folk, flocks, and flowers.

Yet ah! this air I gather and I release
He lived on; these weeds and waters, these walls are what
He haunted who of all men most sways my spirits to peace;

Of realty the rarest-veinèd unraveller; a not
Rivalled insight, be rival Italy or Greece;
Who fired France for Mary without spot.

GERARD MANLEY HOPKINS

For Sidney Bechet

That note you hold, narrowing and rising, shakes
Like New Orleans reflected on the water,
And in all ears appropriate falsehood wakes,

Building for some a legendary Quarter
Of balconies, flower-baskets and quadrilles,
Everyone making love and going shares—

Oh, play that thing! Mute glorious Storyvilles
Others may license, grouping round their chairs
Sporting-house girls like circus tigers (priced

Far above rubies) to pretend their fads,
While scholars *manqués* nod around unnoticed
Wrapped up in personnels like old plaids.

On me your voice falls as they say love should,
Like an enormous yes. My Crescent City
Is where your speech alone is understood,

And greeted as the natural noise of good,
Scattering long-haired grief and scored pity.

PHILIP LARKIN

Lesbos

The Pleiades are sinking calm as paint,
And earth's huge camber follows out,
Turning in sleep, the oceanic curve,

Defined in concave like a human eye
Or cheek pressed warm on the dark's cheek,
Like dancers to a music they deserve.

This balcony, a moon-anointed shelf
Above a silent garden holds my bed.
I slept. But the dispiriting autumn moon,

In her slow expurgation of the sky
Needs company: is brooding on the dead,
And so am I now, so am I.

LAWRENCE DURRELL

Moonrise

I awoke in the Midsummer not to call night, in the white
    and the walk of the morning:
The moon, dwindled and thinned to the fringe of a
    finger-nail held to the candle,
Or paring of paradisaical fruit, lovely in waning but
    lustreless,
Stepped from the stool, drew back from the barrow, of
    dark Maenefa the mountain;
A cusp still clasped him, a fluke yet fanged him, entangled
    him, not quit utterly.
This was the prized, the desirable sight, unsought,
    presented so easily,
Parted me leaf and leaf, divided me, eyelid and eyelid of
    slumber.

GERARD MANLEY HOPKINS

216

The Slate Ode

Two stars coming together—a great meeting,
a flint path from an old song,
the speech of flint and air,
flint and water, a ring with a horseshoe;
on the layered rock of the clouds
a milky sketch in slate—
not the schooldays of worlds
but the woolly visions of light sleep.

We sleep upright in the thick night
under the fleece hat.
The spring runs back whispering into the timbers
like a little chain, little warbler, speech.
Terror and Split write with the same little stick of milk.
Here, taking form, is the first draft
of the students of running water.

Steep goat cities.
The massive layering of flint.
And still the beds,
the sheep churches, the villages.
In the plumbline is their sermon,
in the water their lesson, time wears them fine,
and the transparent forest of the air
has been filled with them for a long time.

Like a dead hornet by the honey-comb
the pied day is swept out in disgrace.
The black night-harrier carries
burning chalk to feed the flint.
To erase day by day the writings
from the iconoclastic board,
and to shake visions, already transparent,
out of the hand like nestlings.

The fruit was coming to a head. The grapes ripening,
the day raging as a day rages.
Knucklebones—a gentle game—
and the coats of savage sheep-dogs, at noon.
Like rubble from icy heights,
from the backs of green icons,
the famished water flows, eddying,
playing like the young of an animal,

and crawls toward me like a spider,
over the moon-splashed crossings.
I hear the slate screech
on the startled crag.
Memory, are those your voices
teaching, splitting the night,
tossing slates into the forests,
ripping them from the beaks of birds?

Only the voice will teach us
what was clawing and fighting there.
And we will guide the callous slate
as the voice leads us.
I break the night, burning chalk
for the firm notation of a moment.
I exchange noise for the singing of arrows.
I exchange order for the fierce drumming of a grouse.

Who am I? No simple mason,
roofer or boatman.
I'm a double-dealer, with a double soul.
I'm the friend of night, the assassin of day.
Blessed is he who called the flint
the student of running water.
And blessed is he who buckled
the feet of the mountains onto solid ground.

Now I study the scratched diary
of the slate's summer,
the language of flint and air,
a layer of darkness, a layer of light.
I want to thrust my hand
into the flint path from an old song
as into a wound, and hold together
the flint and the water, the horseshoe and the ring.

OSIP MANDELSTAM
TRANS. CLARENCE BROWN
W. S. MERWIN

In the Valley of the Elwy

I remember a house where all were good
  To me, God knows, deserving no such thing:
  Comforting smell breathed at very entering,
Fetched fresh, as I suppose, off some sweet wood.
That cordial air made those kind people a hood
  All over, as a bevy of eggs the mothering wing
  Will, or mild nights the new morsels of spring:
Why, it seemed of course; seemed of right it should.

Lovely the woods, waters, meadows, combes, vales,
All the air things wear that build this world of Wales;
  Only the inmate does not correspond:
God, lover of souls, swaying considerate scales,
Complete thy creature dear O where it fails,
  Being mighty a master, being a father and fond.

GERARD MANLEY HOPKINS

Night and Morning

One night of tempest I arose and went
Along the Menai shore on dreaming bent;
The wind was strong, and savage swung the tide,
And the waves blustered on Caernarfon side.

But on the morrow, when I passed that way,
On Menai shore the hush of heaven lay;
The wind was gentle and the sea a flower,
And the sun slumbered on Caernarfon tower.

ANON
TRANS. FROM THE WELSH
BY R. S. THOMAS

Acknowledgements

The editor and publishers gratefully acknowledge the following for permission to include their poems in this selection:

Anvil Press and Peter Levi, 'The Break of Day' and 'A Letter on a Dusky Wet Morning'

Jonathan Cape Ltd and the Estate of Robert Frost, 'Never Again would Birds' Song be the Same' from *The Poetry of Robert Frost* edited by Edward Connery Lathem; and the Society of Authors for the Estate of A. E. Housman, 'Into My Heart' and 'With Seeds the Sowers Scatter' from A. E. Housman's *Collected Poems*

Professor Joseph Clancy, 'From Winter' from *The Earliest Welsh Poetry*, 1970

J. M. Dent Ltd and Trustees of the Estate of Dylan Thomas, 'The Force that Through' and 'A Refusal to Mourn' from *Collected Poems* of Dylan Thomas

The Dublin Institute of Advanced Studies, 'I am Taliesin' translated by Sir Ifor Williams from *The Poems of Taliesin*, 1968

Faber & Faber Ltd, 'Epilogue to *The Orators*' from *The English Auden*, 'May' and 'Fish in Unruffled Lakes' from *Collected Poems* by W. H. Auden and 'Miranda's Song' from *The Sea and the Mirror;* 'A Girl's Hair' by Dafydd ab Edmwnd translated by Gwyn Williams from *Welsh Poems: Sixth Century to 1600*, 1973; 'Lesbos' from *Collected Poems* and 'Seferis' from *Vega* by Lawrence Durrell; 'The Love Song of J. Alfred Prufrock' from *Collected Poems 1909–62* by T. S. Eliot; 'Within the Dream you said' from *The North Ship*, 'For Sydney Bechet' from *The Whitsun Weddings* and 'The Explosion' from *High Windows* by Philip Larkin; 'Ancient Music' and 'River Merchant's Wife' from *Collected Shorter Poems* by Ezra Pound

Rupert Hart-Davis, 'Night and Morning' translated by R. S. Thomas from *Song at the Year's Turning*, 1955

Allen Lane and James MacGibbon, 'Votaries of Both Sexes' and 'Was He Married?' from *The Collected Poems of Stevie Smith*

Macmillan Co of London & Basingstoke, M. B. Yeats and Miss Anne Yeats, 'The Choice', 'Memory', 'A Deep Sworn Vow', 'Three Things', 'After Long Silence', 'An Acre of Grass', 'To a Friend Whose Work has come to Nothing', 'Prayer For My Son', 'All Souls' Night' and 'Politics' from *Collected Poems of W. B. Yeats*

Oxford University Press, 'Low Barometer' by Robert Bridges from *The Poetical Works of Robert Bridges;* 'The Slate Ode' by Osip Mandelstam translated by Clarence Brown and W. S. Merrin from *Selected Poems*, 1973

The Society of Authors and the Literary Trustees of Walter de la Mare's Estate, 'The Hare'

A. P. Watt & Son and Robert Graves, 'Lament for Pasiphaë', 'Dawn Bombardment' and 'Cold Weather Proverb'

Index of Titles of Poems

223

Index of Authors